You Can Get OVER IT

How To Confront, Forgive, and Move On

RICK RENNER

TEACH ALL NATIONS

You Can Get Over It:
How To Confront, Forgive, and Move On
ISBN: 978-0-9779459-2-4
Copyright © 2002
Rick Renner Ministries
P. O. Box 702040
Tulsa, Oklahoma 74120-2040

Published by Teach All Nations
P.O. Box 702040 • Tulsa, OK 74170-2040

New Edition 2012

Editorial Consultants: Cynthia Hansen and Andrell Corbin
Text Design: Lisa Simpson, www.SimpsonProductions.net
Cover Design: Debbie Pullman, www.ZoeLifeCreativeMedia.com

Printed in the United States of America.

Dedication

I dedicate this book to my mother, Erlita Renner,
who taught me to walk in love
and to demonstrate the love of Jesus Christ
by serving others.

Mother, I want to thank you
for giving your life to serve and assist so many people
throughout the years.
I cannot imagine a better example than you
of someone who serves others selflessly.
You have been a godly example
to Denise, my sons, and me.

I love you.

Contents

Everyone Has Opportunities To Get Offended or Upset

*T*he fact that you've picked up this book tells me you are seeking answers about how to deal with *bitterness, resentment,* and *unforgiveness.* Everyone has had to deal with these issues at one time or another. So as we get started, I want you to know first of all that you're not alone in your struggles to combat these internal problems of bitterness and resentment. You also don't need to feel embarrassed about your dilemma because it's something that everyone faces at some point in his or her life. But at the same time, you shouldn't accept unforgiveness as an inevitable part of your life. With the

You shouldn't accept unforgiveness as an inevitable part of your life.

help found in this book, you can walk free of these negative attitudes that have kept you bound.

I urge you to stay with me all the way to the end of this book. I intend to take you on a path that will show you how to permanently *uproot* and *remove* bitterness, resentment, and unforgiveness from your life!

You Can Beat the Temptation of Offense

All temptations can be beaten! You just have to make up your mind that you're going to be the *conqueror* and not the *conquered*! This is certainly true when it comes to conquering the temptation to get upset or resentful toward someone.

You may not have realized it before, but getting hurt and offended is a *temptation*. It's a moment when something happens or a thought enters your mind that induces you to get upset or to become angry.

Those thoughts and emotions act as a stimulant to get you all stirred up. Nevertheless, in that moment, you're consciously aware that you can let the temptation to be offended pass you by, or you can allow the thoughts to fester in your mind and emotions until the offense becomes a major issue. It's a choice you make.

It's similar to a sexual temptation. You can choose to turn and look the other way, or you can dwell on that temptation until it fills your mind and imagination. Likewise, if you choose to meditate on a perceived offense, it won't be too long until the devil convinces you that you've been wronged or treated unjustly and that you have every right to nurse that grudge.

If you choose to meditate on a perceived offense, it won't be too long until the devil convinces you that you've been wronged or treated unjustly and that you have every right to nurse that grudge.

If you don't put the brakes on those thoughts, your relationship with that person or group of people will soon be negatively affected by hurt feelings, offense, and grievances. This is certain to happen, whether the offense is real or imagined. And the truth is, most grievances *are* more imagined than real. Most offenses result from a misunderstanding or miscommunication that is blown way out of proportion rather than a direct attack from others.

The Devil Is a Mind Manipulator

The devil is a master when it comes to mind manipulation. He knows that if he can get you to spend a little time meditating on a wrong that was done to you, that perceived wrong will be blown out of proportion until you finally become ensnared in bitterness, resentment, and unforgiveness.

Remember, Satan (then the archangel Lucifer) was kicked out of Heaven because of his ability to create confusion and discord. Heaven is as perfect as an environment can be. Yet in that perfect environment, Lucifer was able to convince heavenly angels with his smooth but totally slanderous allegations against God. Angels who had worshiped together for eons of time suddenly stood *opposed* to each other over nonexistent issues the devil had conjured up in their minds. Satan was so adept at distorting truth that he was able to lure one-third of them into rebelling against Almighty God!

If the devil is persuasive enough to deceive brilliant, mighty, powerful angels, how much easier do you think it is for him to deceive *humans* who live in a far-from-perfect environment and wrestle daily with their own imperfections and with the imperfections of others? The emotional makeup of human beings makes them even more susceptible to the devil's masterful skills of lying, deception, and manipulation.

Satan watches for the right timing and then strikes at an opportune moment. He waits until you're tired, weary, or exasperated. Perhaps you woke up in a bad mood; someone gave you a "look" you didn't like; or you just started your day off on the wrong foot. Suddenly someone does something totally unexpected that you don't like — something that takes you off guard and by surprise.

At first, you're shocked. Then you start to feel hurt. As the day passes and you keep thinking about what happened, the hurt turns into anger. Before you know it, that event is so exaggerated in your mind, you can no longer see it in its true perspective.

That's when the devil whispers his lies to your mind. He may tell you:

You've been so mistreated. If anyone has a reason to be offended, it's you. No one appreciates you! All you do is give, give, and give. What do you get in return? Nothing! You ought to back out of everything you're doing and just let people sit in their own mess!

After all you've done to show your love and to sacrifice for others, what have others done for you? You ought to just walk out on all these ingrates you've been serving and trying to help. They don't appreciate you anyway!

It's totally understandable that your feelings are hurt. Hang on to this offense, and don't ever let anyone hurt you like this again!

When thoughts like these deluge your mind, you need to know that it is Satan setting a trap in front of you. He is trying to ensnare you so he can cripple you emotionally and cut you off from the people you love. He's trying to get you to bite the bait so he can set the hook!

There Is a Way Out!

You don't have to fall into this trap anymore! If you really want to escape this emotional quandary, there is a way out.

First Corinthians 10:13 promises, "There hath no temptation taken you but such as is common to man: but God is faithful, who will not suffer you to be tempted above that ye are able; but will with the temptation also make a way to escape, that ye may be able to bear it."

This verse says that God will make a way for you to escape *any* temptation that comes against you. This even includes those moments when you're tempted to get upset with someone or to allow your feelings to get hurt.

You don't have to give in to the temptation to become offended. You don't have to feel crushed and hurt when others fail your expectations of them. *You don't have to continue living in a prison of bitterness, resentment, and unforgiveness.*

God Will Provide an Escape for You — IF You Really Want To Be Free

Millions of Christians are held captive by bitterness, resentment, and unforgiveness because they will *not* determine to do what is necessary to live free of offense. As a result, they have no joy, no peace, and no victory in their lives. They may be Christians, but they're miserable because they haven't made the choice to jump through the escape hatch God has provided for them and leave all that negative garbage behind.

God *will* make a way for you to escape, but you are the only one who can make the choice to jump through that escape hatch He has prepared for you.

If you'll say yes to the Lord, He will show you how to live totally free from bitterness and unforgiveness. That's right — you can avoid *every* temptation to take offense. You *never* have to get dragged into destructive emotions, feelings, and attitudes.

> *You can avoid EVERY temptation to take offense. You NEVER have to get dragged into destructive emotions, feelings, and attitudes.*

It's Your Choice

So many Christians are inwardly miserable because they keep pushing the rewind button in their minds. They keep going back and replaying every grievance that was ever done to them. *They have replayed these offenses in their minds over and over again.*

If that describes you, here's what you need to understand: You are the *only one* who can choose to walk away from these deadly attitudes. The moment you make that decision, your journey to freedom has begun!

So today the Lord is asking you:

"Are you going to stay the way you are right now, or are you willing to take the proper steps to escape from this emotional temptation and demonic trap? Are you ready to give up all unforgiveness, laying it at the foot of the Cross so you can walk free? Or will you continue to cling to that resentment and turmoil? Will you remain a hostage to those attitudes that cripple you spiritually, mentally, and physically?"

What is your answer? What are you going to do? God is waiting for you to decide whether you will receive the freedom He is offering you or remain a hostage for the rest of your life. *The choice is yours to make.*

Think About It

An offense may have shaped your past, but you don't have to allow it to define your future. God's plan for you is brighter and better than anything that was damaged, stolen, or lost in your life due to disappointment or any sort of wounding offense.

Are you willing to trust God to help you get past the pain and move forward? What are the ways you can cooperate with Him by adjusting your outlook, attitudes, actions, or words?

Whenever you've been wronged, violated, slandered, betrayed, lied to, rejected, or harmed, that's when you must focus your attention on God's promises to you.

In what way does the offense that challenges you stand in direct defiance to what God has either said about you or provided for you? What specific thoughts have dominated your mind that you need to exchange for *God's* thoughts so you can finally get over whatever the "it" is in your life?

Offense Is a Trap

s long as we live in this world, we're going to have to deal with the potential of being offended. We can't prevent offenses from happening, but we *can* avoid taking offense and getting bitter. Opportunities to get offended will always present themselves to each one of us. In fact, Jesus Himself told us that it would be impossible to avoid offenses because they *will* come (*see* Luke 17:1). Jesus wasn't being the bearer of bad news when He said that — He was just telling us the truth.

So if there's one thing we all need to learn, it's how to deal with people and the offenses that inevitably occur in life. That's why the apostle Paul wrote in Hebrews 12:14: "Follow peace with all men..." That word "follow" is the Greek word *dioko*, which means *to follow*, *to pursue*, or even *to hunt*. The use of this word indicates that peace isn't always easy to come by — we may have to *search* for it. And in our relationships with the more difficult people we encounter in life, we will have to *aggressively* seek peace.

Hebrews 12:14 goes on to say, "Follow peace with all men, and holiness, without which no man shall see the Lord." This verse bothered me for years because it appeared to say that if a person died with bitterness or strife in his heart, he wouldn't go to Heaven. After all, the last phrase says, "without which *no* man shall see the Lord." But when I pulled out my Greek New Testament to look up this word "see," I discovered this phrase could be better interpreted: *"without which no man shall be admitted into the immediate presence of God."* This verse really isn't talking about admittance into Heaven. It's referring to entrance into the presence of God *right now.* In other words, if a person knowingly harbors bad attitudes, strife, or unforgiveness in his heart, those attitudes can set up a roadblock in his life that prevents him from experiencing the power and presence of God right now.

It's so important for you to commit yourself to living FREE *from offense — and to make this commitment* BEFORE *you're faced with the opportunity to become offended.*

We've all faced situations in our lives that greatly challenge us in our commitment to walk free from offense. I don't believe that anyone ever wakes up and thinks, *I fully intend to become offended by someone today!* Offenses tend to catch us by surprise. And if we're not on guard against the temptation to be offended, we can easily fall into the trap of offense.

That's why it's so important for you to commit yourself to living *free* from offense — and to make this commitment *before* you're faced with the opportunity to become offended. If you'll make up your mind and settle the matter ahead of time about how you will and will *not* respond, you won't slip, trip, and get stuck when the trap of offense is suddenly set on the path before you.

The 'Pygmy Pastor'

I want to share a personal story that I'm not proud of, but it's one that will illustrate how offense gets started and how it grows out of control if you don't commit to living free of offense. Something happened between another pastor and me many years ago in the early years of our ministry in the Soviet Union. As a result of my immaturity, I became deeply offended and my behavior ended up becoming just as ugly as the person's behavior that had offended me. I am thankful that the Lord confronted me and required me to repent in a dramatic way — dramatic enough that I would learn the lesson and never want to repeat it again. But before I tell you the story, let me begin by saying that he and I are great friends today and are very thankful for each other!

Soon after our family moved to the former Soviet Union in the early 1990s, Denise and I began broadcasting the first daily Christian TV program in the history of the USSR. After a while, we held a large conference — and to our absolute shock, thousands of people attended the meeting. We saw real New Testament signs and wonders during that conference: Cripples were healed; the paralyzed were restored to health; and the deaf and dumb spoke. It was a miraculous event that caught the attention of the entire nation. During that conference, God asked me, *"What are you going to do with all these people who have been saved this week?"* Of course, I understood from His question that He was calling Denise and me to start our first church where we lived in Riga, Latvia, the capital of a small Baltic republic that had once been a part of the Soviet Union.

At that time, there were only two aboveground churches in Latvia. All of the other churches were underground, concealed from the sight of the KGB. Of these two aboveground churches, one was a traditional Pentecostal church that had the guts and gumption to emerge into public view. The other visible church had been started by that Pentecostal church's former youth pastor. This man just couldn't bear with the religious tradition, so he started his own church and declared that he and his congregation were going to lead the way forward for the next generation of believers in Latvia. At the time God told me to start our own church, this man's church was the most progressive and boisterous church in Riga. As a result, it had grown quickly and made quite a noise within the Christian community.

However, there were things I didn't like about this pastor's church. For example, some of the doctrines he taught back then really rubbed me the wrong way. I didn't believe they were scriptural. I also didn't like his arrogant attitude toward all the other Protestant churches in Riga and throughout Latvia. He had publicly bad-mouthed a lot of the underground churches, as well as the other public Pentecostal church. Hearing someone talk like that *really* irked me. It was true that some of the other churches seemed stuck in the traditions of their past, but their congregations were filled with good, faithful people, many of whom had spent time in prison for their faith. I felt they deserved respect.

But this pastor sincerely believed that all of the other congregations would ultimately merge as a part of his church. So when Denise and I started *our* church, he wasn't very happy about it! We were on TV every day, giving voice to the Gospel in the nation where he wanted, but had not achieved, spiritual dominance. And when our church began to grow quickly, he felt threatened. One day he retaliated and started a war of words. Standing in front of his church, this pastor told his congregation, "I know there is another church in Riga that is growing rapidly. But let me tell you what I think about it — any pastor who is bald [referring to me!] is under a curse of God! Don't go visit a church where the pastor is cursed!"

When I first heard what this pastor had said, I thought it was funny. But the more I brooded on it, the more I began to get angry about the situation. *How dare he say something so stupid to influence and manipulate people!* I fumed. People regularly informed me that this man was continuing to make fun of me for being bald — and was even judging my anointing by virtue of my baldness. I wasn't upset because he said I was bald; I don't care about that. I had been losing hair since I was 17 years old, so that didn't bother me. But his arrogant attitude *did* bother me. And the more I thought about that, the more annoyed I became. This preacher who continually reproached me in public was a short man. So to get back at him for what he'd been saying about me, I began to change the way I referred to him in public, calling him "the pygmy pastor"!

I had allowed myself to take offense at this pastor's words and his judgment of me. As a result, those words began to eat me up on the inside.

I had allowed myself to take offense at this pastor's words and his judgment of me. As a result, those words began to eat me up on the inside. It got to the place where I found myself standing behind my pulpit in my own church, saying something very "unchristlike" about this man to my own congregation. I began, "I understand there is another pastor in town — I'm not going to say his name — who has said that any pastor like me who is bald is under the curse of God. But let me tell you what *I* think…"

I could see Denise squirming in her chair on the front row. I knew she was hoping I'd stop before I said what I was about to say. But I barreled forward full blast and declared, "If you want to know who *I* think is cursed, I think anyone whose growth has been stunted is the one under the curse of God!" Then I threw down the verbal gauntlet: "I want to make it clear today that if anyone is cursed, it's a 'pygmy-sized pastor' on the other side of town, and I recommend that no one should attend his church!"

At that moment, a feud marked by raging carnality erupted between me and this other pastor. Back and forth, we began to publicly rip at each other with our words. It was shameful.

I was ready to keep spewing my ugly words as long as it took to win this feud. Then the Holy Spirit arrested me long enough to pose a question to me: *"Rick, do you want to have revival in your life and in your church?"*

"Yes, Lord, you know I do," I replied.

He asked me again, *"Are you absolutely sure you want revival in your church?"*

I answered, "Yes, Lord, you know I do."

A third time, the Holy Spirit asked, *"How badly do you want revival in your church?"*

I answered, "Lord, you know how desperately I want to see revival. I'll do anything You ask of me if it will bring revival in my church."

That's when the Holy Spirit answered me, *"Then I am requiring you to deal with your wrong attitude toward this man, because this foul attitude in your heart will stop you from experiencing revival."*

'But What About HIM?'

> *The Holy Spirit answered me, "I am requiring you to deal with your wrong attitude toward this man, because this foul attitude in your heart will stop you from experiencing revival."*

"But it was this pastor who picked the fight, not me!" I argued. "Good grief! I was new in town. He could have welcomed and supported me, but instead he called me 'cursed' because I was bald and threatened his people not to attend any services at our church. This pastor has done some *seriously* wrong things against me, Lord!"

Even today — 20 years later — people remember the mud-slinging that took place between this pastor and me back in those days. It was *really* nasty and ugly, yet we were the two largest churches in Riga at the time! The entire scenario was extremely ungodly and out of order.

Then the Lord explicitly told me that I was to go to this pastor and repent for my wrong attitude toward him. So I replied to the Lord, "I have a reason for feeling the way I do toward this man. What about *him*, Lord? What are You going to do about all the wrong things he's said and done against *me*?" (Have you ever said something similar to the Lord when He was dealing with you about your bad attitude toward someone else?)

I'll never forget what the Holy Spirit said to me at that moment: *"I'm not talking to you about this man. I'm talking to you about YOU. I will deal with him for what he's done to you, but right now I'm dealing with you for your reactions to him."*

Isn't it interesting that when God deals with us about our wrong attitudes, words, or actions in a difficult situation with someone else, we so often want to justify ourselves by focusing on what the *other* person did wrong? That's just what Adam did in the Garden of Eden. He blame-shifted and said, "This woman *You gave me....*" when God confronted him about his disobedience. When we do the same, we don't seem to realize that we're actually accusing *God* of being irresponsible for not dealing with the other person instead of us!

> **When God deals with us about our wrong attitudes, words, or actions in a difficult situation with someone else, we so often want to justify ourselves by focusing on what the OTHER person did wrong.**

When you think about it, it's really very arrogant of us to ask the One who sees and knows all things, "Lord, don't You see what that person did? Aren't You aware of what he (or she) said to me?" No matter how hard we try to get God to focus on the other person or to come into agreement with our side of things, He will always, *always* point us back to the wrong motivations of our own hearts, because those motivations are the roots that produce any ugly fruit growing in our lives. Jesus commanded us to produce fruit that remains (*see* John 15:16). However that won't happen unless we guard our hearts and diligently pluck out any seeds of strife before they develop into deep roots of bitterness that can pollute our lives and produce poisonous fruit.

This was the lesson I was about to learn — but I definitely wasn't ready for what the Holy Spirit said next to me! He told me to get in the car, drive across town, go into that pastor's office, get down on my knees in front of him, and repent for every slanderous thing I had heard, believed about him, and repeated to others. *Ugh!* That was *the last* thing I wanted to do, but I *knew* the Holy Spirit had told me to do it.

When the Holy Spirit asked me to go to him and get on my knees in front of him, my first response was, "*NO, I WON'T DO IT!* I'm *not* giving that man the gratification of seeing me on my knees in front of him. I don't want to give him the pleasure!" I was *certain* that the moment I walked out of his office, he would tell everyone, "*RICK RENNER* has bowed before me today!"

For two months, I heard the small, still voice of the Holy Spirit, asking me again and again, *"Are you going to obey Me? Are you going to do what I've asked you to do? Are you going to go to that pastor, get on your knees, and repent for your attitude toward him?"* I argued with the Lord for two months about the matter, but He just kept saying, *"Rick, do you really want revival? If you do, then you have to do what I'm requiring you to do."* It got to the point that the Lord was interrupting my prayer time every day, saying, *"Are you going to obey Me? Are you going to obey Me? Are you going to obey Me?"* The sound of those words was like a roaring in my mind.

"Are you going to obey Me? Are you going to obey Me? Are you going to obey Me?" The sound of those words was like a roaring in my mind.

At last I threw in the towel and gave up! I said, *"Yes, yes, yes — I will obey You!"* So I asked my associate to go with me for moral support, and I drove across town to this man's church office. As I sat across the room from the pastor, we talked about the weather, about politics, about our children. Finally, we didn't have anything else to talk about, and I knew the time had come for me to do what I had come to do. I could get up and leave that room with unfinished business and totally fail this assignment, or I could slip down onto my knees and do what Jesus had asked me to do.

After breathing a deep sigh, I told this pastor, "I'm here today to do something that the Lord is requiring me to do."

He just stared at me, so I continued, "I've heard a lot of bad things you've said about me. I know about some of your doctrines that I find to be very wrong. (At that moment, I began to slip into the accusatory mode and had to deliberately pull out of it!) But I'm not here to deal with you today. I'm here today to deal with me. You have offended me, and ever since, I have believed every negative thing any person has told me about you. Please accept my apology for repeating those things to others. I've been wrong. I have been a source of division. I'm here to ask you to forgive me."

At that moment, I wanted to hear this man respond, "Well, Rick, I've said a lot of bad things about you, it's true. I need to ask you to forgive me as well." That would have made me feel so much better. But instead of apologizing to me or acknowledging that he had done anything wrong, he just stared at me with a look of glee in his eyes. I could see that he was relishing every moment of my contrition.

Then the Holy Spirit said to me, *"Now it's time to get on your knees in front of him."*

I argued inwardly with the Lord. *Please don't ask me to get on my knees!*

But the Holy Spirit quietly spoke to my heart, *"Rick, you need to get on your knees in front of this man to properly ask for his forgiveness."*

So I lowered myself down to one knee, thinking that if I did it halfway, the Lord might be satisfied. But I heard the Holy Spirit say, *"BOTH knees!"*

I knew full well at that moment that if I wanted to please the Lord and experience a freshness of His presence within our church, I had to fully obey Him, no matter how humiliated I felt or how this man responded. I also knew that if I didn't get it right this time, I would have to come back a second time. God would *not* let me off the hook. So I knelt on both knees, looked up at this pastor, and said, "Brother, I repent before God and before you for the ugly attitude and words that I've fostered and perpetuated against you."

That day freedom came into my soul. From that day forward, I didn't care what this man said or didn't say about me. I had done what the Lord required of me, and I was free. Even more, I began to take active steps to really pursue peace with him. Denise and I invited him and his wife to our home for dinners on multiple occasions. I also invited him to speak in our church, and I attended his church conferences. I was *pursuing, following,* and *hunting after* peace with this man. After all, we were pastors of the two largest churches in the city. If nothing else, we needed to be at peace with each other for the sake of Christ's testimony in Riga.

> *That day freedom came into my soul. From that day forward, I didn't care what this man said or didn't say about me. I had done what the Lord required of me, and I was free.*

It took awhile, but later this pastor also acted on what the Lord spoke to *his* heart to do in order to pursue peace with *me*. Since that time, he and I have become very good friends. Today if I visit Riga, we always meet for breakfast and share from our hearts with each other. We have a mutual and genuine respect for one another. The devil had very different plans for our relationship, but we chose to thwart those demonic plans by doing what God told us to do in order to pursue peace with each other.

If you have an offense against someone, you can't wait until the other person takes action. God may require you to be the initiator of peace. In my case, I couldn't wait until this pastor chose to reconcile our relationship before I let go of offense. I had to get over it and step out in obedience to the Lord for the sake of His presence in my own life and ministry.

> *If you have an offense against someone, you can't wait until the other person takes action. God may require you to be the initiator of peace.*

As I look back on that day when I knelt before that pastor in his office, I'd have to say that it was one of the hardest things I'd ever done up to that moment in my life. But I learned a priceless lesson through that experience: The flesh will always want to react when someone hurts or wrongs us. But reacting to carnality with more carnality only escalates the situation into a full-fledged manifestation of strife, creating an atmosphere for every evil work. That's exactly what the enemy wants to happen so he can move in to bring destruction and ruin into the lives of everyone involved.

On the other hand, if we will choose to obey God by responding to an offense in humility and love, we'll not only dismantle the enemy's trap, but we'll also create a platform for God to move on both sides of the situation in a way that will honor Him and promote His purposes.

Seek Peace and Pursue It

Sometimes peace can be gained, but it takes lots of hard work to *maintain* it. There are a lot of people who come to a resolution and finally obtain peace. But because of subsequent circumstances, they get offended once again and lose their hard-earned peace.

That's why we're told in Ephesians 4 that we have to endeavor to keep the unity of the Spirit in the bond of peace (*see* Ephesians 4:3). That word "endeavor" is the Greek word *spoudadzo*, which means *to hasten, to go as fast as you can*, or *to put all of your heart into a pursuit*. This tells us that it will not be easy to maintain peace in our relationships. We'll have to continually work at it.

> *It will not be easy to maintain peace in our relationships. We'll have to continually work at it.*

When the writer of Hebrews 12:14 told us to follow peace with all men and "holiness," he used the Greek word *hagios,* which means *to be separate* or *to be different from the world.* Then the verse goes on to say, "…without which no man shall see the Lord."

That is exactly what the Lord meant when He asked me, *"Do you want to have revival in your life and your church?"* When we harbor wrong attitudes in our hearts, those attitudes restrict us from moving up into higher realms of God's presence and glory. We won't be able to enter into the full dimension of God that's available to us because those negative attitudes will block us from experiencing His anointing.

That's why we are instructed to keep our hearts free of offense. However, to obey that divine command requires spiritual maturity. In fact, the next verse goes on to say, "*Looking diligently* lest any man fail of the grace of God…" (v. 15). That phrase "looking diligently" as used in this verse is the Greek compound word *episkopos*, taken from the Greek word *epi*, which means *over*, and the word *skopos*, which means *to look.* When these two words are compounded, the new word *episkopos* means *one who looks over* or *one who has the oversight of something.* This is a person who has a managerial role or a supervisory position. It is the same word that's translated "bishop" in First Timothy 3:1.

To get the full idea of what this phrase means, you have to stop and think for a moment about the role of a bishop. A bishop is responsible for churches. If he is a good bishop, he makes sure that the churches under his care have his focused attention so they will grow and thrive. If he is a poor bishop, however, he won't pay attention to the condition of those churches, and they will eventually fall apart. But whether he does well or poorly, he must give account to God for what happens in those churches because he is the one responsible for them as their bishop.

Now that same word *episkopos* — when used in the context of *strife, unforgiveness,* and *offense* — is translated as "looking diligently." God is plainly telling us here to act as the "bishops" of our own hearts. Just as a bishop is responsible for what happens in a group of churches, we are responsible for what happens in our hearts. This means we can't blame someone else for what we allow to develop inside our own hearts; God will hold *us* accountable for it.

> *We can't blame someone else for what we allow to develop inside our own hearts; God will hold us accountable for it.*

When people hear this scriptural principle, there's usually someone who will say, "You just don't know what So-and-so has done to me. There's a reason I'm hardhearted and bitter. It's not my fault. I have a reason to be like this." When people talk like that, they are basically deflecting responsibility for their own inner attitudes and attempting to justify their own wrong actions in taking offense.

Since offenses come to all of us, we each will have a "reason" to feel offended at one time or another. But not one of us has an excuse for giving in to that temptation. We have to be careful to *look diligently* to keep our hearts free from offense.

Hebrews 12:15 goes on to tell us why it's so crucial that we obey this command: "Looking diligently lest any man fail of the grace of God; lest any *root of bitterness* springing up trouble you, and thereby many be defiled." This word "root" is the Greek word *pidzo*, which describes *something that is deeply implanted*. This tells us that bitterness is not a superficial issue; rather, it develops deep and entangled roots in our souls. The word "bitterness" is the Greek word *pikria*, which describes *something that is inwardly sour, caustic, or sharp*. It describes a person who is so inwardly sour and bitter that it shows up on his face as a *scowl*.

What is in a person will eventually come out of him. Jesus said, "...Out of the abundance of the heart the mouth speaketh" (Matthew 12:34). It isn't difficult to know what is in people's hearts. Just let them talk, and their own words will give them away. Eventually what is in them will come out of them. The mouth is the great revealer of the heart. In fact, whatever is in a person's heart usually dominates the things he or she talks about, whether good or bad.

The mouth is the great revealer of the heart.

For example, if you were to strike up a conversation with me, you'd find that I talk a lot about Russia. I talk about television in Russia, the church in Russia, all of our outreaches in Russia, and so on. Russia dominates my conversation because it occupies my thoughts and fills my heart. Russia is what I think about, what I meditate on. Russia is the place I've given my life to for the Gospel's sake. That's why it comes out of my mouth.

A person's mouth is the outlet for the overflow of a full heart. Thus, if his heart is filled with bitterness, that bitterness will manifest itself in his life. Its caustic, defiling presence will saturate his attitudes and be conveyed through what he says and how he reacts in different situations. A person cannot conceal what fills him. Eventually it will come out.

So with that principle in mind, ask yourself this: *What does my mouth reveal about the condition of MY heart?*

Every one of us should ask ourselves that question. Whatever we meditate on will take root and produce fruit in our lives. Therefore, we have to constantly be on guard regarding what we allow to dominate our thoughts. God doesn't allow us to justify bitterness in our hearts just because we've been wronged or because we have a "good reason." Those so-called "reasons" are

> *Whatever we meditate on will take root and produce fruit in our lives. Therefore, we have to constantly be on guard regarding what we allow to dominate our thoughts.*

simply traps — designed to hinder or destroy us if we allow them to remain lodged in our minds where they can grow and eventually dominate our thoughts. When we're wounded by some sort of offense, that wound will fester if we leave it unchecked. We must determine to let go of that offense and move forward.

The Solution for Offense

So what's the solution to letting go of offense? Jesus told us clearly in Luke 17:3. He said, "Take heed to yourselves: If thy brother trespass against thee, rebuke him; and if he repent, forgive him."

Jesus started out by saying, "Take heed to yourselves...." That is important instruction, because when you're offended, the first thing you want to do is take heed to your *offender*, not to *yourself*. You want to think about what that person has done and talk about it to *anyone* who will listen to you. You'll want to talk about it over and over, relishing in the sympathy you receive as you defile the hearts and minds of those who hear your words.

Bitterness is messy business. It will stunt your spiritual growth because God's presence absolutely will not rest upon you or cause you to flourish when you're in that poisonous state of mind. That's the reason it's of utmost importance that you obey Jesus' command to *take heed to yourself.*

According to the Greek, a better translation of the phrase "take heed" would be *get a grip on yourself.* That is precisely how you get over issues. It's how you operate as the bishop — *the overseer and guardian* — of your own heart. You get a grip on yourself by ceasing to focus on who offended you. You get a grip on yourself by taking command of your thought life and refusing to indulge in self-pity.

Jesus went on in Luke 17:3 to share the full solution: "...If thy brother *trespass* against thee, rebuke him; and if he repent, forgive him." We'll discuss what this part of the verse means in more detail in Chapter Eight, but let's take a quick look now at what Jesus was telling us to do if we become offended.

> *Get a grip on yourself by taking command of your thought life and refusing to indulge in self-pity.*

Take note of that word "trespass." It's the Greek word *hamartano*, which can denote *to violate a rule*, *to cross a line*, or *to commit a grievance*. If your brother violates you, you are to rebuke him. The word "rebuke" comes from the Greek word *epitimao*, and it means *to forthrightly and directly admonish*. Then if he repents, you are to forgive him. This word "forgive" is the powerful Greek word *aphiemi*. This word means *to permanently dismiss*, *to liberate completely*, *to discharge*, *to send away*, or *to release*. The best modern-day translation of this word "forgive" is *let it go*. Thus, Luke 17:3 could read this way: *"If your brother violates you, be straightforward and deal with it. And if he repents, let it go."*

That is precisely how God has forgiven us. Psalms 103:12 says, "As far as the east is from the west, so far hath he removed our transgressions from us." God is certainly capable of reaching into the past and dragging up our former transgressions, but He will not do that because He has *dismissed* those transgressions from us. He will never pull up a reminder of our sins because He has completely released us from them.

Our carnal nature can have a really difficult time with this concept of letting go of offense. When somebody sins against us, it's easy to wallow in self-pity and start singing that old song, "Nobody knows the trouble I've seen. Nobody knows my sorrow." We can start thinking we're justified in holding on to the offense because we think *no one* has ever been hurt to the extent we have. (Of course, in these moments, we can also conveniently forget the times we may have hurt someone else in that same manner or worse!)

If we don't discipline our flesh to let go of offense and self-pity, it will rule as a dictator in our lives. That's why we have to take our place as the bishops of our own hearts. Just like a child, our flesh needs boundaries and discipline, or it will run rampant over our emotions and thought life. We have to *tell* our flesh what it can and cannot do — how it will and will not feel. We have to rein in our emotions and control our flesh by taking control of our thoughts. The way to do this is with our own words. We have to speak to our minds and emotions. Our own voice is the key to our freedom from the debilitating and defiling oppression of offense.

As the bishop of your own heart, you are the only one who has the authority to rip the root of bitterness and offense out of your heart. Jesus said that we could speak to a mountain and it would be cast into the sea (*see* Mark 11:23). There isn't much need to speak to physical mountains and toss them into the ocean, but a stronghold in the soul is a different matter. Like a mountain, a stronghold can tower over your life and hinder you in so many ways. If you're ever going to be free to move forward and live fully in the power of God, it's up to you to release the offenses that built that stronghold in your heart.

> *As the bishop of your own heart, you are the only one who has the authority to rip the root of bitterness and offense out of your heart.*

Moreover, bitterness doesn't just hinder your walk with God — it also impedes your fellowship with others. The fact is, if you're bound by offense against one person, that bondage will affect your other relationships as well. The poisonous attitudes you carry in your heart against one person will affect how you respond to everyone else.

You may have suffered a hurt or offense in the past that harmed you terribly. In fact, it may have even robbed you of something that can never be returned or restored. But if you refuse to forgive — if you refuse to let go of anger, animosity, and bitterness — that offense will continue to work its destruction in your life. A past-tense problem will become a present-tense issue if you refuse to let go of your bitterness. If you don't get over that past offense, you will give it the power to damage and even destroy your future as you drag it along like a bag of garbage or toxic waste. At some point, you have to just let it go and get over the offense for your own benefit.

Whatever may have happened to you in the past or whatever offense you may be holding against someone else right now, I want you to know that you can walk free. You just have to make the decision to exercise your authority over your own heart. Remember, you can't be offended without your own consent. Someone can certainly commit an offense against *you* by speaking or acting inappropriately or unkindly toward you without your provocation. But you cannot be offended unless you *take* the offense to yourself. You always have a choice.

You cannot be offended unless you TAKE the offense to yourself. You always have a choice.

When someone commits an offense against you and you're sorely tempted to "take it," the very first thing you need to do is go to the Lord. Get a grip on yourself as you allow the Lord to deal with you. Let go of the offense that's trying to get a grip on *you*.

Jesus commands you to forgive your offender. The tough part comes when someone commits the same offense seven times in a day and each time repents for what he's done — and you're commanded to forgive him every time! To forgive a person once or twice in one day for committing the same offense would be challenging enough. But seven times in one day? That seems almost impossible to the natural mind! No wonder the apostles exclaimed, "Lord, increase our faith" (*see* Luke 17:5)!

And Jesus didn't stop there! He took this issue of forgiveness even further in Mark 11:25 (*NKJV*) when He said, "And whenever you stand praying, if you have *anything* against *anyone*, forgive him, that your Father in heaven may also forgive you your trespasses." In other words, forgiveness in its highest form is unconditional. As was true in my experience with the "pygmy pastor," God requires all of us to forgive those who offend us, regardless of what the other party in the situation decides to do.

Jesus expects us to be mature and to forgive no matter how other people behave. Remember, the word "forgive" is that Greek word *aphiemi*, which means in modern terms *to let it go*. If your offender turns to you seven times in a day and says, "Please forgive me — I repent," Jesus expects you each time to let go of the offense. Rather than be held hostage by what someone has done to you — or what you may *think* that person has done to you — Jesus says, *"Get a grip on yourself and let it go."*

Perhaps the person who offended you didn't intend to do so, even though you think his actions were deliberate. Or perhaps the offense was a matter of carelessness or insensitivity. Whatever your offender's intention or motivation was, *you* are the one who must decide whether you will permit the offense to hold you captive — or you will determine to let it go.

The only way you can dismiss, release, and let go of an offense is to get into the presence of the Lord and let Him help you. Just come to Him and say, "Lord, I'm not willing to be bound by this offense. I refuse to be imprisoned by these feelings of hurt, rejection, or humiliation. Right now before You, I choose to let it go." That choice is the first important step toward living a life free of offense.

In future chapters, we will talk about steps that must be taken on the other side of that choice. There *is* a way to uproot and remove bitterness and unforgiveness from your life once and for all!

Think About It

We are instructed not to give place to the devil through anger (*see* Ephesians 4:26,27). Are you dealing with a situation that repeatedly tempts you to become angry? That's a sure sign the devil is seeking to find a foothold in your life.

What are some practical ways according to godly wisdom that you can seek peace and pursue it in this situation that the enemy is trying to use against you?

When you're concerned about what others think of you, you've exalted self-importance and public opinion above *God's* opinion in your life. When that happens, a spirit of pride is setting you up for a fall.

Take some time to examine your own heart. In what areas are you willing to humble yourself — to lay down your right to be considered "right" where you were called wrong, or to be vindicated if you were harmed or humiliated? What attitudes, actions, words, or "hardness of heart" are you willing to repent of in order to experience freedom in your fellowship with the Holy Spirit?

CHAPTER

Jesus Understands
Your Emotions,
Frustrations, and Temptations

*I*f you've ever been controlled by hurt feelings and offenses, you know it's a miserable state to be in. So it's important to be honest with yourself if you want to learn how to walk free from offense in this life. Take a few moments to ponder these questions:

- When someone does something that's disappointing to you, how successful are you at dealing with it without taking offense or nursing hurt feelings?

- Is there one particular person who can easily throw you into emotional turmoil that tears you up on the inside?

- Do you find that the devil uses one person or a particular situation over and over to steal your peace and joy?

- Is there a person in your life whom you love but whose insensitivity to your feelings frequently hurts and upsets you?

- Do you harbor ill feelings toward someone? Do you wish you didn't feel the way you do about him or her?

- Are you emotionally paralyzed by what someone has done to you or failed to do for you?

- Are you free from offense, or are you a prisoner of hurt feelings?

- Do you allow offense to roll around in your head and emotions until it finally begins to steal your peace and get you upset?

- Have you tried unsuccessfully to conquer bitterness in prayer? Have you been unable to fully forgive certain people in your life for the offenses they committed against you?

We've all been offended from time to time by something someone said or did or by what he or she *didn't* say or do. Sometimes we're even tempted to get offended by a mere look someone gives us. Offense is something *everyone* has to deal with at one time or another.

Jesus Is Touched
With the Feelings of Your Infirmities

Jesus Christ empathizes with every temptation and struggle you face in this life. He identifies and sympathizes with you. He has compassion for you about what you're feeling and the situation you're facing.

Hebrews 4:15 says, "For we have not an high priest which cannot be touched with the feeling of our infirmities; but was in all points tempted like as we are, yet without sin." This verse declares that when Jesus walked on the earth, He was God in the flesh. Yet He still faced *every* temptation you and I face in life.

This is one reason Jesus understands the emotions, frustrations, and temptations you face in life. He has been where you are. He has felt what you feel. He has overcome the temptations you are now trying to overcome.

Hebrews 4:16 says we have a priest who is "...touched with the feelings of our infirmities...." That's why the next verse urges us, "Let us therefore come

Jesus understands the emotions, frustrations, and temptations you face in life. He has been where you are. He has felt what you feel.

boldly unto the throne of grace, that we may obtain mercy, and find grace to help in time of need."

If Jesus was really tempted in all points as you are, it means:

- If you're tempted to steal, Jesus was tempted to steal too.

- If you're tempted to lie, so was Jesus.

- If you're tempted sexually, Jesus was also confronted by sexual temptation.

- If you're tempted to wear your feelings on your shoulder and get them hurt all the time, Jesus was tempted to feel this way as well.

- If you're tempted to hate and to hold a grudge, Jesus was tempted in exactly the same way. (Just think how you might be tempted to feel if Judas had betrayed you!)

- If you're tempted to take offense, Jesus was also tempted to be offended.

- If you're tempted to give up and quit, Jesus was tempted to give up and quit too.

There's no need to feel too embarrassed to go to Jesus. If anyone can understand what you're going through right now, *it's Jesus*! He has been tempted in all points just like you, yet He never succumbed to temptation. Because of what Jesus went through, He understands your dilemma. He is familiar with disappointment. He has experienced the temptation to get frustrated and upset. That's the reason Hebrews 4:16 says to come *boldly* to the throne of grace!

As One who has faced every temptation you personally face, Jesus is on your side and is standing by to assist you.

As One who has faced every temptation you personally face, Jesus is on your side and is standing by to assist you. When you come to Him, you *will* obtain mercy and find grace to help in time of need.

Jesus Was Tempted
To Get Offended and Upset

You may ask, "Rick, how do you know that Jesus was tempted to get offended and upset or to allow His feelings to get hurt?"

I know because the Bible very clearly states that Jesus faced *each* temptation you and I face in life. Jesus never fell into one of Satan's traps, but He definitely faced these frustrations. If Jesus *hadn't* been tempted by every temptation as we are, He wouldn't be able to understand us and serve as our Great High Priest.

I can only imagine the frustration Jesus must have felt in the Garden of Gethsemane. He had invested three and a half years of His life into His disciples. Now for the first time, He needed *them*. So He asked three of His disciples to pray for Him during His hour of temptation (*see* Matthew 26:37-45). Jesus asked them for only one hour of prayer, but instead of praying, they fell asleep. He returned a second time and pleaded with them to pray with Him, but once more they fell asleep. For a third time, Jesus came and besought His disciples to pray, but again they fell asleep on the job.

What if you had been in Jesus' shoes that night? What if you had given three years of your life to these disciples — but when you finally asked them to help *you* for once, they kept failing you again and again?

It would be normal for a person in this situation to be tempted to become resentful, upset, or even offended. Anyone in that position would be tempted to think, *How dare you sleep on the job after all I've done for you! I'm sorry I ever did anything for you bunch of ingrates!* But Jesus never fell into that trap. Instead, as He hung on the Cross, He prayed, "…Father, forgive them…" (Luke 23:34).

People's Inconsistent Behavior Can Be Surprising!

Do your best to understand people, but never be too shocked if people do something that takes you by surprise!

People can be quite a mystery. You finally think you have them all figured out, and then they do something that totally blows your mind! You never would have dreamed in a million years that they'd do something so crazy or inconsistent. That's why if you're going to live a happy life, you have to learn how to forgive and overlook people's inconsistencies, lack of commitment, unfaithfulness, temper tantrums, and mood swings — as well as all the other defects connected with being a human being.

Honestly, there are days I don't even understand my *own* moods. Therefore, I know I have to show mercy when I see others act differently than I expect them to. When I'm tempted to get upset with Denise, my sons, or my associates in the ministry, I stop to remind myself that I'm not perfect either. I'm sure there are moments when these same people are just as bewildered by me as I am by them!

- Do you always understand your own moods?

- Do you always have a grip on your own emotions?

- Do you ever do anything that's inconsistent with what you know is right?

- Do you ever fall short of the standards you set and demand of those around you?

I can't complain too much about others being a mystery because I'm such a mystery to myself sometimes! Oh, how I long for the day when I walk in the Spirit 100 percent of the time. Unfortunately, it looks like that won't happen until my ———————————— mortal flesh puts on incorruption!

We have to maintain an attitude of forgiveness and extend the same mercy to others that we expect them to extend to us.

When we receive our glorified bodies and go to Heaven, all our inconsistencies, mood swings, double standards, and complex emotions will be gone. We'll be in good moods forever! Until then, we have to maintain an attitude of forgiveness and extend the same mercy to others that we expect them to extend to us.

Forgive me for being so gut-level honest, but until that day when the entire Body of Christ sees Jesus face to face, believers will experience moments when:

- Husbands' behavior upsets their wives.

- Wives make their husbands angry.

- Children disappoint their parents.

- Parents lose their tempers with their kids and hurt their children's feelings.

- Friends are nowhere to be found when they are desperately needed.

- Employees betray their fellow employees to get a better job or promotion.

- Employers play favorites with employees rather than dealing fairly and justly as they should.

- Church members talk about their pastor behind his back.

- Pastors occasionally repeat what was told to them in confidence, wounding and hurting the church member who privately confided in him.

Even Christians who spend hours in prayer, read the Word, pray in the Spirit, and seek to live a holy life sometimes get in the flesh, doing and saying things they later regret. *It's just part of being human.*

Is This an Opportunity for the Holy Spirit To Deal With YOU?

If you're going to get upset every time someone says or does something beneath your expectations of that person, you'll live your life constantly bothered and frustrated. Similarly, if you lose your peace every time someone *doesn't* do what you expect of him or her, you're going to live an up-and-down roller-coaster existence!

Rather than focus on the inconsistencies and flaws of others, why not look in the mirror and let the Holy Spirit deal with *you*? It may be that God is using the people who may have wronged you to expose something in your own character that needs to change!

That's why it's so important to always ask yourself, *What has this situation revealed about me?*

- *Do I lack patience?*

- *Do I lack kindness?*

- *Do I lack temperance?*

- *Am I unforgiving?*

- *Am I a grudge-holder?*

- *Am I intolerant?*

- *Am I a complainer?*

- *Am I judgmental?*

- *Am I unsympathetic?*

- *Am I critical and fault-finding?*

If a particular relationship or situation has revealed a weakness in your own character, just determine to stop looking at the faults of others and let God's Spirit teach you to overcome your own exposed faults.

Galatians 5:22 says, "But the fruit of the Spirit is love, joy, peace, longsuffering, gentleness, goodness, faith, meekness, temperance: against such there is no law." A mature Christian must learn to let the fruit of the Spirit operate in him or her regardless of the situation.

When your relationships with others are going great — when you have no challenges, problems, or conflicts with anyone — it's easy to be kind, loving, and longsuffering. But the real proof of spiritual maturity isn't measured by the moments when your flesh is comfortable. True spirituality is revealed by those situations that rub your flesh the wrong way! In those moments:

- Are you able to crucify your flesh?

- Are you able to esteem others above yourself?

- Are you able to think of the interests and concerns of others?

In order to live a fulfilling Christian life, you must develop the fruit of the Spirit in your spiritual walk. If you try to base your joy and happiness on other people, you'll *never* be happy. You'll end up feeling hurt, disappointed, wounded, and angry much of the time because no person will ever be able to do enough to keep you happy. On the other hand, when you cultivate your relationship with the Holy Spirit and develop the fruit of the Spirit in your life, you can be joyful and content in any environment. Your happiness will come from within and won't be affected by people or by outside circumstances.

Some have tried to find their meaning and fulfillment in other people for so long and have been let down so many times that they have become bitter and resentful. If this situation persists over a long period of time, these bad attitudes will begin to color their entire perspective of life and make them completely miserable — even if they call themselves "Spirit-filled Christians."

If you've harbored these types of unhealthy attitudes, you must allow them to be *recognized, uprooted,* and *removed* by the Spirit of God. Otherwise, they will begin to produce vile fruit that has the power to socially isolate you and emotionally immobilize you for the rest of your life.

Left untended, the poison of bitterness, resentment, and unforgiveness becomes like a terminal disease. These deadly attitudes eventually begin to eat away at your insides, turning you bitter and destroying every relationship in your life.

A True-Life Example

Let me tell you of a true-life example that illustrates the destructive effects of bitterness, resentment, unforgiveness, and offense.

I'm thinking of a precious woman in the former USSR whom I have known for years. She is one of these emotional prisoners about whom I am writing. She may be free to walk the streets of her city, but she is just as bound as any person I've ever ministered to in a real prison.

There are *reasons* why this woman is bitter and resentful. Her early life was filled with hurt and abuse. But she has never been able to forgive those who hurt her and, as a result, has been held captive to her bitterness for many years.

She was just one of millions who were mistreated during the Soviet years. Many people could tell a similar story, but they have learned to forgive, get over the wrongs done to them, and move on. This woman has never been able to let the past be buried. Captivated by these hurts, she now lives in a very lonely and solitary world. Week after week, she sits alone in the balcony of the Riga church, not allowing anyone to touch her, talk to her, or get close to her in any way.

Resentment and *unforgiveness* have caused this woman to prejudge everyone who tries to draw near to her. Her past wounds have become an excuse for not trusting people and for accusing the entire Body of Christ of being hypocrites. But what she accuses others of is *exactly* what she has become.

Her whole appearance and speech has become stern and harsh. Her body is filled with crippling, debilitating arthritis. She is the precise reflection of the hate she carries in her soul.

This may sound like an extreme case — I wish it were. But sadly, it's a very real scenario for many believers. The truth is, the Body of Christ is filled with people who carry scars from the past that adversely affect their present lives and relationships.

Have you ever been abused, hurt, let down, wounded, deserted, or betrayed by your spouse? Stabbed in the back by fellow church members? Or rejected by your parents, family, or friends? If you can answer *yes* to any of these questions, you know how the devil can use such an experience to debilitate you.

But it's time to move on and let the past be the past.

If you carry wounds, bruises, and scars from previous hurts and offenses, you don't have to carry them anymore. *You don't have to live today with the residual effect of what the devil did to you yesterday.*

Jesus Understands and Wants To Set You Free

As we've already discussed, everyone will have opportunities to get upset or offended, and the devil will make sure that you're no exception! It's important that you know how to respond to these opportunities so you don't get entangled in the devil's snares.

In the next chapter, I will explain to you *exactly* how the devil operates in the realm of your emotions. If you understand the tactics he uses, you can thwart his attacks before he sows bad seed into your soul. This next chapter may be the life-saving revelation you've been crying out for God to send you!

Before you blame others for their failures or point your finger at the devil, go to the mirror of God's Word and ask yourself: How DO I NEED TO CHANGE?

However, let me first encourage you to do one more thing. Before you blame others for their failures or point your finger at the devil, go to the mirror of God's Word and ask yourself:

- *How do I need to change?*

- *How can I become more understanding?*

- *How can I develop more patience in my life?*

- *How can I extend mercy to those who hurt me?*

- *How can I correct weak areas in my character that have been exposed by these circumstances?*

Jesus understands your struggles with bitterness and resentment. He had to overcome the same type of temptations Himself. So the next time you're feeling hurt and offended because of other people's behavior, get quiet in your heart and listen to the voice of His Spirit. Ask Him to reveal to you what needs to change in your own life. That's the first step in walking out of the bondage of bitterness into the freedom of forgiveness!

Think About It

Consider the humility of Jesus. He remained silent when He was reviled, and He prayed for those who deliberately sought His harm.

When people are inconsistent or disappoint you, do you respond to them like Jesus responds to you when *you* are inconsistent or disappoint Him?

You can't control others, but you can and must control yourself.

What are your trigger points — those areas in which you are easily and often tempted to become offended or upset? Is there someone in your life that regularly "presses your trigger"? The next time that happens, what can you do differently to avoid reacting in your own practiced pattern of offense? And what do you need to do to get over it — for good?

CHAPTER

How the Devil
Operates in the Realm
of the Mind and Emotions

I want to help you understand how the devil works in the realm of the mind and emotions. What I am about to tell you is simple, but it's also life-changing and revolutionary. If you grab hold of these truths, they can set you free from the devil's lies forever!

Let me begin by saying that the devil has no right to operate in your life unless you open a door for him to come in and do his business. Therefore, when you keep wrong attitudes out of your life, you make it very difficult for the devil to find an entrance into your family, friendships, relationships, health, finances, ministry, or business.

When the devil can't come in the front door, he often seeks a way to get in through the *back* door. One back door he uses is a heart infected with bitterness, resentment, and unforgiveness. These attitudes create an entrance for Satan to intrude right into the middle of your most vital relationships. And believe me, keeping the devil *out* of your relationships is far easier than trying to *remove* him after he's already found his way inside!

> *Keeping the devil OUT of your relationships is far easier than trying to REMOVE him after he's already found his way inside!*

However, if the devil has already gotten a foothold in any area of your life through these destructive attitudes, I'm here to tell you that *you can still walk free*!

Standing Against the Wiles of the Devil

In Ephesians 6:10-18, Paul explicitly tells us how the devil operates. This passage of Scripture is extremely important for you to know and understand. (I recommend that you read my book, *Dressed To Kill*, which deals expressly with the issues of *spiritual warfare* and *spiritual weaponry*.)

In Ephesians 6:11, Paul writes, "Put on the whole armour of God, that ye may be able to stand against the wiles of the devil." I want you to especially pay attention to the phrase "the wiles of the devil." Understanding the meaning of this phrase will give you insight into the way the devil attempts to operate in a person's life.

Three other key New Testament words to understand as well are the words "devices," "deception," and "devil." Once you see how these words relate to each other, I believe a veil will be lifted and the light of revelation will shine in your heart, causing you to understand how the devil tries to operate in most people's lives, *including your own*.

Stay with me now as I take you on a Greek word study you will never forget!

What Are the 'Wiles' of the Devil?

The word "wiles" is taken from the word *methodos*, which is a compound of the words *meta* and *odos*. The word *meta* is a preposition that means *with*. The word *odos* is the word for *a road*. When the words *meta* and *odos* are compounded into one word, as in Ephesians 6:11, the new word *methodos* literally means *with a road*.

You've probably already figured out that the word *methodos* is where we get the word "method." Some translations actually translate the word *methodos* in Ephesians 6:11 as the word "method," but this English word is *not* strong enough to convey the full meaning of the Greek word *methodos*.

Let me make the meaning of this word real simple for you. The most literal meaning of the word "wiles" (*methodos*) is *with a road*. I realize that this meaning may initially seem a little strange. But when you connect this meaning to the devil as Paul does in Ephesians 6:11, it begins to make sense. It means that *the devil travels on one road, one lane, one path, or one avenue.* In other words, *he possesses only one approach to you.*

I realize that many believers think that the devil has all kinds of imaginary ways to find access into their lives. However, the word *methodos* tells us that the enemy *doesn't* have a whole bunch of tricks in his bag. He only has *one approach* or *one way* to get into a person's life.

Let me give you an example of what I mean. If you're going to take a trip, the logical thing for you to do is to get a map and chart your journey to your destination. You don't take just any ol' road; rather, you strategize to find the best and fastest way to get where you're going. *Right?*

It would be pretty foolish for you to jump in the car and take off with no sense of direction. Taking any ol' road could lead you in a multitude of wrong directions. It's just better to use a map and stay on track.

This is precisely the idea of the word *methodos*. The devil isn't wasting any time. He knows where he wants to go. He has chosen his destination. Instead of messing around on a bunch of different routes, he has mastered the most effective way to get where he wants to go.

The devil is *not* a mindless traveler. When he arrives at his place of destination, he has one main goal he wants to accomplish: to wreak havoc and bring destruction. That's what the enemy attempts to do whenever and wherever he shows up.

Therefore, we must ask: *"Where is the devil traveling, and what does he want to do once he gets there?"*

> *The devil is NOT a mindless traveler. When he arrives at his place of destination, he has one main goal he wants to accomplish: to wreak havoc and bring destruction.*

The Devil's Destination and Desire

I believe Paul answers the question about Satan's destination in Second Corinthians 2:11 when he says, "…we are not ignorant of his [Satan's] *devices*."

Pay careful attention to the word "devices" in this verse. It is the Greek word *noemata*, a form of the word *nous*, which is the Greek word for *the mind* or *the intellect*. Thus, in one sense Paul is saying, *"…we are not ignorant of Satan's mind"* or *"…we are not ignorant of the way Satan schemes and thinks."*

But the word *noemata* also denotes Satan's insidious plot to fill the human mind with *confusion*. There is no doubt that the mind is the arena where Satan feels most comfortable. He knows if he can access a person's mind and emotions, he will very likely be able to snare and entrap that individual.

This Greek word not only depicts Satan's scheming mind, but also his crafty, subtle way of attacking and victimizing *others'* minds. The word *noemata* can even carry the notion of *mind games.* This means you could translate the verse, *"...we are not ignorant of Satan's mind games."*

I personally like this translation because I believe it identifies the primary destination of the devil — *to get into a person's mind and fill it with lying emotions, false perceptions, and confusion.* It was for this reason that Paul urged, "Casting down imaginations, and every high thing that exalteth itself against the knowledge of God, and bringing into captivity every thought to the obedience of Christ" (2 Corinthians 10:5).

The devil loves to make a playground out of people's minds and emotions! He delights in filling their perceptions and senses with illusions that captivate them, paralyze them, and ultimately destroy them — *just like the woman I told you about in the previous chapter.*

> **If you're going to beat the devil at this game, you have to put all your energy into taking EVERY thought captive to the obedience of Christ.**

Rather than fall victim to the devil's attacks, you must make a mental decision to take charge of your mind and emotions. If you're going to beat the devil at this game, you have to put all your energy into taking *every* thought captive to the obedience of Christ. And once you make the decision to do it, you must *stick to your resolution.* If you're not really committed to seizing *every* thought the devil tries to inject into your mind and emotions, he'll strike you again!

For example, the devil may try to tell you, *You're a failure. You're a failure. You're a failure.* These mental assaults will produce nothing as long as you resist them. But the day you begin to believe those lies and perceive them as truth, you're in trouble.

If you don't quickly abort the devil's deceptive thoughts, it won't be long until your faith gives power to that lie and causes it to become a bona fide reality in your life. *You will become a failure!*

Mark 11:23 Works for the Devil Too

Mark 11:23 is a powerful verse about faith and confession that believers claim and use. *But the principle in this verse works for the devil too.* The verse says, "For verily I say unto you, That whosoever shall say unto this mountain, Be thou removed, and be thou cast into the sea; and shall not doubt in his heart, but shall believe that those things which he saith shall come to pass; he shall have whatsoever he saith."

According to what Jesus taught in this verse, you can bring to pass whatsoever you *say* and *believe in your heart*. For instance, if you believe in your heart that Jesus purchased your healing and you put your *heartfelt faith* together with the *confession of your mouth*, you can literally bring that healing into manifestation in your physical body.

Creative power is released when the heart and mouth get in agreement! That's why you must be careful about what you believe in your heart and say with your mouth, because when your heart and mouth get "in sync," it makes things happen!

This *heart–mouth combination* works both positively and negatively. It can bring about the manifestation of healing to your body, salvation to your family, prosperity to your business, and growth to your church. *But the devil also knows how to use this principle against you!* He knows that if he can fill your mind and heart with lies that you believe and then coax you to start confessing those lies with your mouth, you'll make those evil images come to pass!

That's the reason the devil wants to fill your mind with deceptive thoughts and to paint his lies so vividly on the "movie screen" of your mind. It's also the reason he assaults your mind and emotions *again, again, and again.* Satan knows if he can get you to embrace these evil mental images, you'll start speaking them out of your mouth — *and if you start speaking them, you'll bring them into manifestation.*

Out of the Abundance of the Heart

Jesus said, "…out of the abundance of the heart the mouth speaketh" (Matthew 12:34). *In other words, whatever is in your heart is eventually going to come out of your mouth!*

Because great power is released when your heart and mouth start working together, it's extremely important that you put the right things *in* your heart. When you bring your heart and mouth into agreement with God's Word, you are moving into the realm of creative faith.

Because great power is released when your heart and mouth start working together, it's extremely important that you put the right things IN your heart.

Mark 11:23 promises that whatever you believe in your heart and say with your mouth *will* come to pass. But as I said before, this doesn't just apply to Bible promises; it applies to *anything* you believe in your heart and say with your mouth. So if the devil can get you to believe and say wrong things, your own heart and mouth will cause those killer confessions to come to pass.

The devil wants you to repeat every stupid thing he puts in your head. By repeating it out loud, you are helping him build a STRONGHOLD in the realm of your mind.

I know it's hard to control your mouth sometimes. But when you start to "run at the mouth" and speak out whatever thought the devil puts in your mind, you're playing with *fire*!

It's a scientific fact that when you speak something *out loud*, those words are verified and empowered in your mind. That's why the devil wants you to repeat every stupid thing he puts in your head. By repeating it out loud, you are helping him build a *stronghold* in the realm of your mind.

An Emotional Puppet or a Renewed Mind?

Once the devil has established a stronghold in your mind, it's just a matter of time until he starts pulling your emotional strings. He wants to make you an *emotional puppet* of his own design!

You see, whoever controls your mind also controls your emotions. And whoever controls your emotions has the supreme power to affect your self-image, your marriage, your friendship, your relationships, the way you project yourself to others, and so on.

This is another reason why it's so important for you to spend time in the Word of God. As you spend time meditating in the Word, your mind is *renewed* to God's way of thinking (*see* Ephesians 4:23; Colossians 3:10). God's Word brings a supernatural cleansing that washes your mind and emotions from the contamination of the world, the memories of past bad experiences, and the lies the enemy has tried to sow into your brain.

When you make it a priority to fill your mind with truth from God's Word, you make it difficult for the enemy to penetrate your mind. And if he can't penetrate your mind, he can't touch your emotions either. On the other hand, your own failure to fill your mind with God's Word could result in catastrophe as every area of your life is left vulnerable to Satan's assaults.

A person whose mind is renewed to the Word of God is strengthened and undergirded inwardly. He is harder to deceive because his strong foundation of truth repels the enemy's attacks.

Satan knows that empty heads are easy to deceive. That's why he just loves it when he finds a believer who has made no effort to fill his or her mind with truth from God's Word. The enemy has found another empty head just waiting for someone to come along and fill it — and he's happy to oblige!

> *When you make it a priority to fill your mind with truth from God's Word, you make it difficult for the enemy to penetrate your mind.*

Someone Is Going To Control Your Mind, So Who Is It Going To Be?

Your mind is going to be filled with *something*, so you may as well choose the right thing to fill it. Who or what is going to control your mind? *God and His Word? Or the enemy and his lies?* Your choice in this matter will determine your successes or your failures in life, so make sure you choose wisely.

I want to give you an example of what happens when people let the enemy take control of their minds and emotions. Let's talk about the very basic example of marriage.

Many marriages fail because of lies the devil pounds into the minds of one or both spouses. For example, the devil may whisper to the wife, *Your marriage is in trouble. Your marriage is in trouble.* At first, the wife recognizes this thought as a lie from the enemy. She knows that although her marriage isn't perfect, her relationship with her husband is strong and their love for each other is solid and true. Yet the enemy continues to pound away at her mind — *striking, battering, beating,* and *hammering* her mentally and emotionally with lying allegations:

- *This relationship can't stay this strong forever.*

- *This is too good to be true.*

- *This marriage won't last long.*

- *This dream is about to burst.*

The wife may know these thoughts are preposterous. But if she doesn't *rebuke* and *reject* these doubt-filled thoughts, they will begin to take her to the next level of mental accusations, such as:

- *He can't love you this much.*

- *He is interested in someone else.*

- *He doesn't send you flowers anymore.*

- *He looks at other women with interest.*

- *There is something wrong.*

- *Your marriage is in serious trouble.*

- *It's time for you to get a lawyer!*

The moment husbands and wives begin to dwell on that kind of devilish propaganda, the door is thrown wide open for the enemy to really begin pounding their minds relentlessly. At that point, they will live with a torrent of tormenting and harassing thoughts about their marriage until they put their foot down and command the devil to *stop*!

The devil is extremely proficient at bombarding people's minds and emotions with his lies and deceptions until they finally accept those lies as truth. In fact, he has had a high degree of success with the human race through his strategy of mind control. That's the reason multitudes of people take medication for depression and spend loads of money buying self-help books.

> *The devil is extremely proficient at bombarding people's minds and emotions with his lies and deceptions until they finally accept those lies as truth.*

As a believer, however, there is never a need for you to be overcome by the devil's intimidations, suggestions, or lies. He may hammer as vigorously and persistently as he can, but Satan is simply not able to penetrate your life when you're safeguarded by *the shield of faith* and your mind is fortified by *the helmet of salvation* (*see* Ephesians 6:16,17).

What Does the Name 'Devil' Mean?

The name "devil" comes from the Greek word *diabolos*. But this Greek word *diabolos* is much more than a name — *it's a job description*! It tells you *how* the devil operates and *what* he wants to try to achieve in your mind, emotions, and, ultimately, in every area of your life, *including your relationships.*

The word *diabolos* is a compound of the words *dia* and *ballo.* The word *dia* means *through*, as in the sense of *someone piercing through something from one side to the other* and depicts Satan's ability *to pierce* or *to penetrate.* The word *ballo* means *to throw*, such as in *throwing a ball or rock.* It describes *a fast-forward, hurling motion.* It's the same Greek word used in John 13:2 to describe that moment when the devil swiftly *injected* a seed of betrayal into Judas' heart. (You will read more about this in the next chapter.)

When the words *dia* and *ballo* are compounded, the word *diabolos* is formed — the New Testament word for *the devil.* It literally describes *one who repetitively hits something again and again and again — until finally that object is so worn down and defeated that it can be pierced and penetrated.*

An example of this in the natural realm would be the collective effect of water dripping on a rock. One little drop by itself isn't powerful, but when thousands of little water droplets drip *again*, *again*, *again*, and *again* over a prolonged period of time, the force of their combined dripping has the potential to drive a hole all the way through solid rock!

That's why you need to fortify yourself with the Word of God and surround yourself with people of faith, especially when you're tired and exhausted. The devil revels in attacking when you're in a weakened condition. He cherishes those moments when he finds you alone and worn out. When you're *fatigued*, *wiped out*, *and drained of all energy*, the enemy knows that you are more susceptible to the lies and images he wants to feed you.

> *Fortify yourself with the Word of God and surround yourself with people of faith, especially when you're tired and exhausted. The devil revels in attacking when you're in a weakened condition.*

Daniel 7:25 explicitly tells us that the devil loves to "wear out the saints." He does this by continually feeding his cunning words of deception to our minds and emotions. His goal is to break down our resistance so he can fill our minds with accusatory assertions about ourselves or someone else.

Therefore, if you know you're in a weakened condition, you must be more watchful about thoughts that pass through your mind. When you are weak, tired, and worn out, it's much easier to see things amiss, to hear things wrongly, and to perceive things incorrectly.

I rarely engage in conversations about difficult topics when I'm exhausted because that's one of those times when I don't see, hear, or perceive things well. I have seen the devil take advantage of these moments in my life too many times, arousing my temper and causing me to get agitated.

Since I know this about myself, I try to stay out of intense conversations when I'm extremely tired and therefore more easily tempted by the devil. It's better for me, and everyone else involved, to wait until I have regained my strength before we tackle the matter at hand.

Don't Give the Devil a Chance To Get in the Middle of Your Relationships

So often we open the door for the devil and invite him right in by having quarrels and disagreements at moments when we're weak or tired. Sure, problems need to be discussed. But they *don't* need to be discussed when we're so exhausted that we can't see straight! That's one of those moments when we are perfect prey for the devil's attacks.

Think for a moment. How many friendships could have been spared if all parties involved had taken a little time to rest before they expressed their disagreements and differences? How many husbands and wives could have avoided saying ugly, debasing, hurtful words to each other if they had gone separate ways for a couple of hours to pray and assess the situation before they continued their dialogue?

When *pessimistic, disapproving, cynical, mocking, sarcastic,* or *disparaging* thoughts start to flood your mind about someone, it's best for you to back away from those thoughts for a while and give yourself a break. That string of negative thoughts should be a warning flag to you that the accuser is trying to wedge his way into your mind and emotions. Spend some time getting quiet before the Lord, and allow Him to give you *His* perspective of the situation.

When the devil's mental attack begins, it may sound like this:

- *Why do you let those people treat you the way they do?*

- *They don't appreciate you, so why do you keep doing all the things you do for them?*

- *It would be better for you to go join another church where you'd be recognized and honored!*

- *Stop serving your ungrateful spouse — he (or she) doesn't deserve someone as kind and giving as you are!*

If you don't turn a deaf ear to what the devil is telling you, it won't be long until those lies begin to sprout and send roots of bitterness deep inside your head and heart. And if you don't allow the Holy Spirit to help you uproot and remove those lies, they'll soon affect your friendships and relationships.

A Relationship-Breaker
From the Beginning of Time

The devil has tried to wedge his way into relationships since the very beginning of time.

First, he stirred up strife between one-third of the angels and God.

Second, he made his way into the Garden of Eden and tried to ruin the relationship between God and man.

Third, he wedged his way between Cain and Abel — two blood brothers — and succeeded in causing mankind's first murder.

From beginning to end, the Bible makes it clear that the devil has always been a *relationship-breaker.* Since that is the case, it's imperative that you learn how to protect yourself against his attacks.

Are Your Relationships a Joy or a Curse?

Relationships can be a *joy* or a *curse* in your life, and you are the one who decides which they will be. There are two key factors that determine the nature of your relationships: 1) how you nurture them, and 2) how you deal with conflict.

Most conflicts stem from petty disagreements that aren't even important. Oh, how the devil loves to uses unimportant clashes to destroy healthy relationships!

Here's what makes it even worse: Frequently while the fight is on and emotions are engaged, those who are arguing can't even remember how the fight got started in the first place! *This should tell the parties involved how unimportant the conflict really is.*

There are two key factors that determine the nature of your relationships: 1) how you nurture them, and 2) how you deal with conflict.

These disruptions create tensions that rob us of our joy and make us nervous and sick from being upset all the time. That's why Jesus warned us, "The thief cometh not, but for to steal, and to kill, and to destroy..." (John 10:10).

You see, the enemy wants to *steal* the fellowship you enjoy with that person, *kill* the sweet friendship you once had, and totally *destroy* any prospect of restoring that relationship. *Don't let him do it.* Use what you know about how he operates to stand against his wiles and deceptions and walk free of bitterness and strife!

Think About It

A lie or false accusation is at the root of every offense. In any given situation, the offender or the offended must believe and act on some sort of lie or distortion before an offense can even take place.

Sift through the meditations of your heart today. Have you allowed a belief contrary to God's truth to wield its deceptive influence? Has the enemy succeeded in using that lie to distance your heart from God or from others?

If you knew a predator of some sort was stalking you, studying your habits in order to gain access to your property, you would most likely take specific and aggressive precautions to ensure your protection.

What precautions do you take on a regular basis to protect your mind, emotions, and relationships from spirits of wickedness that seek access to steal peace, kill effective communication, and destroy unity between you and the people in your life?

The Friend
Who Became Jesus' Betrayer

I want to show you how Satan penetrated one of Jesus' closest associates and friends. This chapter will help you understand the devil's strategy to use people close to you to inject hurt and betrayal into your heart so the pain can then fester into bitterness.

Judas Iscariot was Jesus' close associate for three and a half years before he became a betrayer. In fact, he was so close to Jesus that he became the *treasurer* for Jesus' ministry (*see* John 12:6). This gives us insight into the kind of relationship that existed between Jesus and Judas.

We may assume that as treasurer for Jesus' large ministry, Judas probably had many lengthy conversations with Him to discuss finances. Jesus must have trusted Judas and his administrative abilities to put him in charge of such a vital part of the ministry. *Yet this trusted friend and associate became the very one Satan used to betray Jesus.*

How Did One of Jesus' Disciples Become His Betrayer?

Have you ever wondered how it was possible for someone so close to Jesus to become His betrayer? *How did the devil slip through the cracks and so affect Judas' attitude that he would sell out the Son of God for 30 pieces of silver?*

As we have already seen, the devil is looking for a way to penetrate every good relationship. No story demonstrates this better than the story of Judas Iscariot. Let's take a look at one particular event where the devil obviously found a point of penetration into Judas' life.

In John 12, Jesus and His disciples were having dinner in the home of Mary, Martha, and their brother Lazarus, whom Jesus had raised from the dead. This family was very close to Jesus during His earthly ministry.

Martha showed her love and gratitude for what Jesus had done for them by preparing a large meal for Him and His disciples. Mary showed her love by bringing Jesus an extremely expensive gift. Lazarus showed his love by simply sitting with Jesus at the table as a close friend. This is an interesting demonstration of how different people express their love in different ways.

Mary's Lavishly Expensive Gift

The Bible tells us that the expensive gift Mary brought Jesus was ointment of spikenard — an entire pound of it! Spikenard was one of the most expensive perfumes that existed at that time. Let me tell you a little about spikenard so you can appreciate what Mary did for Jesus that day.

Spikenard was an uncommon perfume extracted from grasses that grew in the country of India. Once the juices were squeezed out of the grass, they were dried into a hard, lardlike substance.

Turning that lardlike substance into perfume was a very lengthy and costly process. Add to this the cost of transporting it from India to other parts of the world, and you can see why this particular perfume cost so much money.

Spikenard was so expensive that few people could buy it; most had to buy one of the many cheap imitations available. But the word used in John 12:3 tells us that Mary didn't bring Jesus a cheap imitation; she brought Jesus *the real thing* — an ointment so valuable, it was normally reserved and used only as gifts for kings and nobility. *This was the gift Mary brought to Jesus.*

We can learn more about the value of Mary's gift in John 12:3, where it says the ointment was "very costly." This phrase "very costly" is from the Greek word *polutimos*, a compound of the words *polus* and *timios*.

The word *polus* means *much* or *great*. The word *timios* means *to honor, to respect*, or *to attribute worth to something*. When these two words are compounded, the new word describes *something that is of great worth* or *something that is of considerable financial value*.

We'd call this "top-of-the-line" giving!

Mary's Expression
of Appreciation for Jesus

As remarkable as it is that Mary even possessed a gift this valuable, it is even more amazing that she brought it to Jesus. And even more phenomenal than that is what Mary did with this perfume once she brought it!

John 12:3 says, "Then took Mary a pound of ointment of spikenard, very costly, and anointed the feet of Jesus...." Everyone must have gasped when they saw Mary take the lid off that bottle, tip it downward, and begin to pour that precious ointment on Jesus' feet. This kind of perfume was not normally used on feet. Mary's action would have been considered a horrible waste in most people's minds, but that's not how she saw it. Mary loved, appreciated, and valued the feet of the Master!

Isaiah 52:7 describes why Mary felt this way: "How beautiful upon the mountains are the feet of him that bringeth good tidings, that publisheth peace; that bringeth good tidings of good, that publisheth salvation; that saith unto Zion, Thy God reigneth!" No other feet in the entire world were more beautiful to Mary than the feet of Jesus. Jesus had changed her life and brought her brother back from the dead (*see* John 11:32-44). For her, every step Jesus took was *precious, honored,* and *greatly valued.*

For three and a half years, Jesus had taught, "For where your treasure is, there will your heart be also" (Matthew 6:21; Luke 12:34). Mary's actions revealed her heart as she poured her *most valuable treasure* onto the feet of Jesus. John 12:3 tells us that she "...wiped his feet with her hair...." In other words, after Mary poured the spikenard onto Jesus' feet, she reached up to her head, untied her long, beautiful hair, and gathered it in her hands. Then she leaned down and began to wipe Jesus' feet dry with her hair.

> *Mary's actions revealed her heart as she poured her MOST VALUABLE TREASURE onto the feet of Jesus.*

In the days of the New Testament, a woman's hair represented her glory and honor. The apostle Paul referred to this in First Corinthians 11:15 when he wrote that a woman's hair was a "glory" to her.

For Mary to undo her hair and use it as a towel to wipe the feet of Jesus was probably the greatest act of humility she could have shown. She was demonstrating how deeply she loved and greatly valued Jesus. I can imagine the tears that streamed down her cheeks as she touched those precious feet. In total humility, Mary dried Jesus' feet with the glory and honor of her hair. John 12:3 tells us that "...the house was filled with the odour of the ointment."

An Opportunity for Bitterness, Resentment, and Offense

However, the devil was able to use Mary's act of humility and love toward Jesus to create an opportunity for bitterness, resentment, and offense to take over in Judas' mind. Judas indignantly asked Jesus, "Why was not this ointment sold for three hundred pence, and given to the poor?" (John 12:5).

Judas said the spikenard could have been sold for "three hundred pence." What is a "pence"? The Greek word for a "pence" is *denarius*. In that day, a Roman *denarius* was *one day's salary*.

When Judas announced that the spikenard could have been sold for "three hundred pence," he was saying that Mary's perfume was worth *300 days' worth of salary*. In other words, this was an *extremely expensive* gift! But Jesus explained to Judas that Mary was anointing Him for the day of His burial. He also told Judas to leave Mary alone and not to disturb what she was doing (*see* John 12:7).

Jesus' Words Could Have Offended Anyone Listening

Then Jesus continued, saying, "For the poor always ye have with you; but me ye have not always" (John 12:8). This answer could have easily been misinterpreted. Those who were listening could have thought Jesus was saying, "Quit talking about poor people! You'll always have the poor, but you won't always have *Me*!"

Jesus had certainly demonstrated His compassion toward the poor during His three years of ministry. Nevertheless, His words to Judas could have sounded arrogant and insensitive to those who were listening.

Did Judas misinterpret Jesus' response that evening? Did he perceive Jesus to be arrogant and insensitive to the needs of poor people?

The disciples watched as this valued treasure was poured out on Jesus' feet. It looked like superfluous waste and excess. It's obvious that Judas considered it to be exactly that.

What about all the poor people who could have been helped with the money from the sale of that perfume? Weren't they more important than this expensive demonstration of love?

As you will see in John 13:2, the devil found entrance into Judas' heart during this dinner at the home of Martha, Mary, and Lazarus. Somehow that evening, the enemy had found an open door — a way to penetrate Judas' mind.

How Did the Devil Get a Foothold in the Heart and Mind of Judas?

How did the devil get inside Jesus' inner circle of friends to try to abort His ministry? Did Judas become *offended* with Jesus? Is this how the devil was able to start pounding away at Judas' mind until he was finally lured into betraying Jesus?

> *How did the devil get inside Jesus' inner circle of friends to try to abort His ministry?*

John 13:2 tells us something very powerful about the way the devil established a foothold in Judas' heart and mind that night. It says, "And supper being ended, the devil having now put into the heart of Judas Iscariot, Simon's son, to betray him."

Especially notice the phrase, "...the devil having now *put into* the heart of Judas Iscariot...." The words "put into" come from the Greek word *ballo*, one of the two words that make up the compound word *diabolos*, the name for the "devil," that we discussed earlier. This word *ballo* means *to throw*, *to cast*, *to thrust*, or *to inject*. It carries the idea of *a very fast action of throwing, thrusting, or injecting something forward* — such as the throwing of a ball or rock or the forward thrusting of a sharp knife.

Below are some examples of the word *ballo* in the New Testament. Look carefully at how this word is used in each of these various references.

- **Matthew 9:27; Mark 2:22; Luke 5:37**

  The word *ballo* is used in these verses to depict *putting wine into new wineskins*. The emphasis is on *putting wine into a new bottle* or *making a deposit into a receptacle*.

- **Matthew 25:27**

  The word *ballo* is used to depict *putting money into the hands of investors* or *depositing money into a place that will earn interest for the investor*.

- **Matthew 27:6**

  The word *ballo* is used to depict *putting or depositing money into the treasury or bank*. Again, the emphasis is on *making a deposit*.

- **Mark 7:33**

  The word *ballo* is used to depict *Jesus putting His fingers into the ears of a deaf man*. Because this word is used, it tells us that Jesus didn't take a lot of time to tell the deaf man what He was about to do. Instead, He *abruptly inserted* His fingers into the man's ears to initiate the man's healing.

- **John 5:7**

  The word *ballo* is used when the crippled man states *he has no one to put him into the pool when the water is stirred.* Here the word *ballo* means *to cast, throw, or forcibly hurl forward into the pool so quickly that he gets in before anyone else.*

- **John 12:6**

  The word *ballo* is used to describe *Judas' responsibility for the money that was put into the bag or the treasury of Jesus' ministry.* The force of the word *ballo* indicates *a deposit made so deep that it isn't retractable.* As treasurer, Judas alone had the authority to remove the money once it had been *deposited* into the bag.

- **John 18:11**

  The word *ballo* is used when Jesus commands Peter to *put his sword back into its sheath in the Garden of Gethsemane.* The use of the word *ballo* indicates Jesus *abruptly* commanded Peter to *put* his sword *away* and to do it *quickly.*

- **John 20:25**

  The word *ballo* is used when Thomas says *he must put, thrust, or insert his fingers into the nail prints of Jesus' hands, feet, and side to believe.* The primary idea of *ballo* in this verse is *to insert into* or *to thrust into.*

In all these examples, the word *ballo* carries the idea of *quickly inserting, injecting, thrusting, putting into, forcibly hurling, or deeply embedding something into an object.* The usage of this word tells us that when the devil decided to "put into" the heart of Judas the idea of betraying Jesus, he knew he had to *act fast.*

When Satan finally penetrated Judas' mind and emotions with this seed of betrayal, he injected it so hard and fast that it became *deeply embedded* or *lodged* in Judas' soul. Therefore, John 13:2 could be translated:

- *"...the devil having now thrust into the heart of Judas Iscariot...."*

- *"...the devil having now inserted into the heart of Judas Iscariot...."*

- *"...the devil having now forcibly hurled into the heart of Judas Iscariot...."*

- *"...the devil having now embedded into the heart of Judas Iscariot...."*

There is no doubt that the word *ballo* means the devil *quickly seized* an opportunity and *injected* a seed of betrayal into the heart of Judas Iscariot. The moment Judas became offended by Jesus' statement in John 12:8 ("…The poor always ye have with you; but me ye have not always"), the devil found his entry point into Judas' heart. At last, Satan had discovered a way to penetrate Jesus' inner circle!

> *Judas was used as Satan's instrument because he allowed the enemy to drive a wedge between himself and Jesus.*

Judas was used as Satan's instrument because he allowed the enemy to drive a wedge between himself and Jesus. Rather than let the disagreement go and forget about it, Judas allowed the issue to become a big deal in his mind — something blown all out of proportion. He let the devil mess around in his mind and emotions and didn't take every thought captive — and as a result, the incident tainted his view of Jesus and adversely affected their relationship.

Has this ever happened to you?

- Have you ever had moments when you were tempted to think badly of someone?

- Did you know that you faced a choice — that you could either overlook what the person did to offend you or let the offense get lodged deep down inside you?

- Were you aware that the devil was trying to sow a seed of discord into your soul — that he was attempting to make you take offense or get upset?

- Have you experienced times when the devil's plan worked because you made the wrong choice, allowing your mind to be seized by bitter, resentful thoughts?

Well, that is exactly what happened to Judas Iscariot.

When Satan Tried To Use Me as a Betrayer

I'll never forget the time in my life when Satan tried to use me as a betrayer. I was a young man, working as an associate pastor in a large Southern Baptist church. The pastor I assisted was a wonderful man who had taught me and unselfishly poured his heart and life into me. He loved me as if I were his own son.

Then one day, I became offended by something this pastor did. (You can read more of this testimony in my book, *Ten Guidelines To Achieve Your Long-Awaited Promotion!*)

In retrospect, I see that what happened was minor and shouldn't have affected me at all. (Isn't it interesting how well we all see things in hindsight?) But the devil had been waiting for the perfect opportunity to attack my mind and try to ruin our relationship. At that moment, I was his *perfect prey*. The incident that had offended me became a major issue in my mind. I didn't realize that I was allowing this over-exaggerated issue to become an open door for the devil.

It's amazing how quickly a dart of the enemy can be thrown into your heart. Equally amazing is the speed in which just one of his evil darts can change your perspective of someone you used to honor and respect!

In a matter of seconds, my entire view of this man had become adversely affected. Like the dripping of water on a rock that I wrote about earlier, the devil began to repeatedly strike my mind with accusations against that pastor. The enemy would whisper to my mind:

- *He's so arrogant and proud!*

- *If other people saw what you see, no one would attend this church. He doesn't really love his people!*

- *He doesn't appreciate you. He doesn't deserve to have you serve on his staff. Leave him!*

- *The people in this city need a pastor who really loves them. It's time for you to leave him and go start your own church!*

I didn't realize that deception was creeping into my heart. I had fallen into the devil's trap and didn't know it. What I ended up doing to that pastor was blatantly wrong. However, at the moment it was happening, I really believed I was doing the right thing.

Questions To Ask When Something
Is Becoming a Major Issue to You

Whenever something becomes a major issue between you and someone else, you would be wise to back up and reexamine what you are upset about. Often the person you're upset with is someone you love and need in your life. Therefore, ask yourself these questions:

- *Do I want to let the devil build a wall between me and this person over something that won't even matter a year from now?*

- *Do I really think this person intended to hurt me?*

- *Wouldn't it be better to forgive him (or her) and preserve our relationship, which has taken so long to build?*

> *Ask yourself: Do I want to let the devil build a wall between me and this person over something that won't even matter a year from now?*

- *Is what happened really so serious, or am I blowing the whole incident out of proportion?*

- *Have I ever been guilty of committing the same offense against someone else?*

I've discovered from my own experience that the devil is constantly seeking opportune moments to wedge bad feelings between people. He is a master at embellishing real or imagined offenses in people's minds until they become inflated and larger than life. And he knows just when to spring an attack! That's why it's so important to stay alert to Satan's devices so you won't get caught unaware in the trap of offense.

Focus on the Condition of Your Own Heart

Let me give you an important piece of advice: If you will concentrate your attention on the condition of your own heart, you'll be too busy to focus on what you think is happening in other people's hearts!

The condition of our hearts is serious business. Hebrews 12:15 tells us that it is our responsibility to oversee what goes on inside our own hearts, minds, and emotions. As long as our hearts and minds are free of bitterness, resentment, and unforgiveness, the enemy will find it harder to penetrate us or to access our relationships. We don't ever have to make the mistake that Judas did!

> **The condition of our hearts is serious business.**

Think About It

The mind-numbing pain from betrayal in an intimate relationship is designed by the devil to strip your confidence and disrupt your life on the deepest level — from how you view your worth to how you value others. Jesus was wounded in the house of His friends (*see* Zechariah 13:6), yet He refused to be distracted. From the garden of Gethsemane to Golgotha's hill, Jesus demonstrated that prayer was central to His response toward disappointment, betrayal, false accusation, and deliberate attack.

Think about it. Whom do you need to forgive? In what practical ways can you commit yourself to God and to prayer about this situation in a way that's deeper or different than what you've done in the past? Have you avoided prayer because you're actually angry with God regarding what has happened? Are you so disappointed with yourself that you aren't willing to try or trust your own choices?

Some betrayers are strategically launched into your life by the enemy to detonate like a time-released bomb. Others, however, are created through the course of offense that your own behavior may have perpetuated.

Have you, by your own conduct, caused a loyal friend to turn into a staunch enemy? Has your own behavior provoked a friend to stumble and be ensnared by the trap of bitterness? Do you justify behavior that tempts other to become offended with you? Think about how you can amend your ways to prevent the pain of another damaged or destroyed relationship — and the need to repent later for your part in the outcome.

You Are the Bishop of Your Own Heart

*S*o how do we uproot and remove the devilish "weeds" of bitterness, resentment, and unforgiveness from our lives? To answer that question, let's go back to our earlier discussion of Hebrews 12:15 and look further at what it teaches us.

This verse tells us, "Looking diligently, lest any man fail of the grace of God; lest any root of bitterness springing up trouble you, and thereby many be defiled." Let's focus once more on the words "looking diligently" in this verse. As discussed earlier, this phrase comes from the compound Greek word *episkopos*, which means *to look over* or *to take supervisory oversight* and is translated "bishop" in First Timothy 3:1. A bishop has *oversight* or *responsibility* for a group of churches. As the chief overseer for those churches, it's the bishop's responsibility to *watch*, *direct*, *guide*, *correct*, and *give oversight* to the churches under his care. As long as he serves as bishop, he will be held responsible for the good *and* the bad that occurs under his supervision.

The word *episkopos* in Hebrews 12:15 alerts you and me to the fact that we are the bishops of our own hearts. It's our responsibility to *watch*, *direct*, *guide*, *correct*, and *give oversight to* what goes on inside our minds and emotions. We must ultimately answer for both the good and the bad that occurs within our thought life.

Why do I stress this point again? Because we are so often tempted to blame our bad attitudes and bitterness on what other people have said or done. But the truth is, we are responsible for our own emotions and reactions!

> *If a person does something that has the potential to offend us, God holds us responsible for whether or not that offense takes root in us.*

If a person does something that has the potential to offend us, God holds *us* responsible for whether or not that offense takes root in us. We can choose to let the offense sink into our souls and take root, or we can opt to let it bypass us. We're not able to control what others do or say to us, but we *are* able to control what goes on *inside* of us.

It's that "inside" part — *the part we control* — that God will hold us responsible for. Why? Because we are charged with a personal responsibility to *oversee* what goes on inside our souls.

You have the last word. You're the one who decides whether or not that wrong settles down into your soul and starts to take root in your emotions.

You may say, "But, Rick, what that other person did to me was so wrong. It hurt me so deeply! It made me so mad!"

Anger is an emotion that comes and goes. You *choose* whether or not irritation turns into *anger*, anger into *wrath*, wrath into *resentment*, resentment into *unforgiveness*, and unforgiveness into *bitterness*. You *choose* whether these foul attitudes and emotions take up residency in your heart or are booted out the door!

When the devil comes to tempt you with an annoying, hounding thought about the person who offended you, you have a choice at that moment whether or not to let it sink in. You're the *only* one who can give permission for these attitudes to settle in and take up residence in your mind and emotions.

So quit saying, "I'm this way because So-and-so did this to me" or "I can't help the way I feel." *Those are all lies*. If you're filled with bitterness, resentment, and unforgiveness, you permitted the devil to sow that destructive seed in your heart and then you permitted it to grow. Remember, you're the bishop of your own heart!

Keep the Weeds Out of Your Own 'Garden'

There is only one reason weeds grow out of control in a garden — because no one took the proper time and care to uproot and remove them.

When the garden is choked by weeds, the gardener can't complain, "I just don't know how this happened! How did this occur right under my nose?" It occurred because he was being irresponsible with his garden. If he'd been exercising the proper amount of diligence, he would have known that weeds were about to get the best of him. The gardener's *lack of diligence* is the reason his garden got into this mess!

Hebrews 12:15 says, "Looking *diligently....*" It takes *diligence* to keep your heart in good shape. The only way you can stay free of the weeds the devil wants to sow in your "garden" is to be attentive, careful, thorough, and meticulous about the condition of your own heart.

So don't make excuses for any rotten attitudes that might be filling your thoughts about the people who supposedly did you wrong. Even if they really did commit wrongs against you, it's neither necessary nor beneficial to permit the devil to fill you with putrid feelings of bitterness, resentment, and unforgiveness. You can get over it and move on! You don't have to let offense fester inside you until you are inwardly eaten up by its bad memory.

As long as you blame everyone else for the bitterness that rages inside, you'll never be free from the destruction it causes in your life. If you're going to get over the offense and walk free of your emotional prison, you must start by accepting responsibility for your own heart.

You are the only one with the authority to permit bitterness, resentment, and unforgiveness to take root and grow in your heart. You have the power of the Holy Spirit at your disposal to uproot and remove those spiritual weeds — *if* you really want them removed!

If you're going to get over the offense and walk free of your emotional prison, you must start by accepting responsibility for your own heart.

God Holds Us All Responsible

If someone deliberately sows bad seeds in our "garden" in an effort to hurt or destroy us, *God will deal with them.* But if we know bad seed is sown in our hearts and we just ignore it, allowing it to take root and grow unchecked, *God will deal with us.* We can't answer for the actions of other people, but we *will* answer for our inward responses to what others have done to us.

Let me share an example about a brother in the Lord who deliberately tried to injure our ministry. To this day, I don't understand why this man did what he did — and in retrospect, I don't think he knows why he did it either. But what he did at that time was very hurtful to the outreach of our work, and the devil tried to use his actions to make me *bitter*. When it happened, I knew I had to make a choice *to forgive* or *to hold on to the offense.*

The more I thought about what the man had done to us, the more upset I became. Soon my negative feelings toward him grew deeper and deeper into my soul. My thoughts toward him were bitter — and these unchecked thoughts began to affect my spiritual life. I smiled and spoke politely to him when in a situation that demanded I speak to him, but inwardly I *resented* this man with every bone of my body.

> *I was so angry at what the man had done to us that I allowed every negative word and imagination to freely pass through my mind, and I inwardly agreed with everything the devil said about him.*

The devil began pounding my mind. I knew it was the devil, but I was so angry at what the man had done to us that I allowed every negative word and imagination to freely pass through my mind, and I inwardly agreed with everything the devil said about him.

After allowing these devilish thoughts to have free course in my mind for a while, I came to the place where this man *disgusted* me. The very thought of him perturbed me. As far as I was concerned, he was a *no-good, low-down, useless bum* parading about in the disguise of a brother and man of God. When others spoke highly of him, it irritated me. I wanted everyone to know the truth as I knew it. I wanted people to know what a *wretch* he was!

I found my mind dominated by this man and what he had done to us. Denise pleaded with me to give the matter to the Lord, but I told her, "He's done us wrong, and I have every right to feel the way I do!"

I finally had to admit that I was in deep water spiritually one day when I gathered my sons together to pray with me. I told them that we were going to ask God to take the man's life. I wanted the Lord to deliver me from ever having to deal with this man again! I was jolted awake to the dangerous condition of my heart when our eldest son Paul said, "Daddy, I'm sorry, but I don't think we can agree with this prayer. We've never prayed for God to kill someone." That was the moment I realized that this man was no longer the problem. *I was the problem!*

I was filled with bitterness because I had chosen to let bitterness have a place inside me. God's way was forgiveness, but I had *permitted* and even *cultivated* my offended feelings toward this brother because of what he had done to me.

- I knew I needed to forgive.

- I knew I needed to let go of the offense and let it die.

- I knew I was consumed with wrong attitudes.

- I knew I was hurting myself more than I was hurting anyone else.

- I knew my feelings of hostility weren't healthy.

- I even knew that my flesh was throwing a pity party in the midst of trying to justify my wretched feelings about this man.

I was overflowing with anger and resentment about what the man had done to us. Because of these bitter attitudes that were festering inside me, I was in no position to stand in judgment of someone else. What he had done couldn't have been any worse than the ungodly emotions I was harboring against him. His sinful actions were outward, to be seen by all. On the other hand, mine were inward and hidden, and they were tearing me up on the inside!

One day the Lord spoke to me, saying, *"Rick, I'm going to hold you responsible for the bitterness you've allowed to work in your heart toward this man. Yes, what he did was wrong — and I will deal with that. But if you don't deal with your own heart and get rid of this bitterness toward your brother, I will deal with YOU!"*

Stay Out of the Judgment Business

Regardless of what that brother had done to me, I knew that bitterness and offense were *not* to have a place in my heart.

Neither was it my place to "play God" and decide who needed to be judged.

Our flesh is always tempted to judge others for their failures. *But judgment is not our business.* It's God's place to decide whose actions and motivations are right or wrong — *not ours.* When we move ourselves into a position of deciding whose motives are right or wrong, we have assumed a responsibility that does *not* belong to us. According to Romans 12:19, it's *God's business* to deal with those who have done us wrong, not ours. We aren't even supposed to touch it!

The longer I've walked with the Lord, the more I've come to realize how difficult it is to figure out my own heart, let alone everyone else's heart as well! In this particular case, it was *my* heart that was filled with a root of bitterness; therefore, I needed to deal with myself. No one could make that choice for me. God's Spirit made it very clear that it was my responsibility to uproot and remove that garbage from my soul. God would empower me to do it, but He wouldn't do it without my cooperation. *This is a very important principle for you to understand.*

We are all occasionally tempted to become bitter or offended with husbands, wives, siblings, parents, and brothers or sisters in the Lord. *But we must understand that offense is a killer of our spiritual lives.*

> *We must understand that offense is a killer of our spiritual lives.*

I understand that it's disappointing when your husband is harsh, unkind, and inconsiderate. It's frustrating when your wife nags at you all the time. It's hurtful when your children are disrespectful and rebellious. It's disappointing when your friends aren't there when you need them. It's agonizing when a person betrays you. It's heartbreaking when you put your whole heart into a relationship and it doesn't turn out the way you hoped. It's devastating when someone else gets the promotion you've been waiting to receive.

But rather than let the devil use these adversities to fill us with resentment and unforgiveness, we must do everything we can to forgive, let go of the offense, and keep our hearts free! Rather than blame our negative attitudes on others, we must take personal responsibility for our thoughts and uproot bitterness from our souls before it produces destruction in our spiritual lives.

Let God's Grace Help You!

God's Spirit will speak to your heart and warn you to deal with bitterness before it becomes deeply rooted in your soul. This divine pleading is God's grace trying to help you overcome the situation before it becomes more serious. Don't ignore that work of grace!

Whether or not you live free from bitterness and unforgiveness depends on your willingness to let God direct your life and change what's wrong in your thinking. He wants to help you, but He *can't* help you if you won't listen or if you refuse to do what the Word tells you. Your cooperation is *required* in order for God's grace to accomplish its full work inside you.

So pay close attention when the Holy Spirit speaks to your heart about letting go of an offense. Obey that inner prompting, and deliberately choose to forgive what your offender has done. God wants to deliver you from bitterness and resentment before you sink so deeply into Satan's trap that it becomes extremely difficult for you to get out of it.

> *Pay close attention when the Holy Spirit speaks to your heart about letting go of an offense. Obey that inner prompting, and deliberately choose to forgive what your offender has done.*

Stay sensitive to the Holy Spirit, and allow His grace to have its full effect in your life. Then bitterness and resentment won't have an opportunity to become deeply rooted inside your heart.

- *You know the Holy Spirit's voice.*

- *You know when He's telling you to forgive.*

- *You know when God's grace is trying to help you.*

If you'll just do what God is telling you to do, you'll be spared from the devastating effects of bitterness, resentment, and unforgiveness. But if you choose to hold on to those destructive feelings and *ignore* what God is trying to do to help you walk free of offense, you will fall short of the grace of God. That's exactly what Hebrews 12:15 is talking about when it says, "Looking diligently, *lest any man fail of the grace of God....*"

I'm thinking of a woman in our church who had suffered many rejections during her lifetime. She had been rejected by her mother, her father, her husband, and even by her children.

When God first brought this woman to our church, we knew He had brought her to us for her full restoration. *God's grace* was on her in a powerful way to bring her to a place of personal change and of forgiveness toward those who had offended her through the years.

Day by day she'd come closer and closer to forgiveness. Then something would happen that would trigger her old feelings of bitterness. *God's grace* was there to help this woman overcome those bitter feelings, but time after time she rejected that grace and reached back to grab hold of that bitterness again. I am amazed at the incredible grace that was available to help her change — *but she rejected it over and over again.*

Today the woman still attends church, but she is not a free person. She still carries the same old, deep scars she has always carried. It isn't that *God's grace* was unavailable to change her. Divine grace was mightily available, but she didn't allow it to work in her life. Therefore, *she failed the grace of God.*

Don't let that be your story. You are the personal caretaker of your own heart, and God will hold you responsible for the attitudes that linger inside you. His grace is available to help you change. You don't have to be imprisoned in bitterness, unforgiveness, or resentment any longer.

If these destructive inward feelings have established a stronghold in your life, make the choice to reach out and grab hold of God's grace. His grace will break those chains off of your soul and set you free from the prison of offense that has held you captive for so long!

> *You are the personal caretaker of your own heart, and God will hold you responsible for the attitudes that linger inside you. His grace is available to help you change.*

You Have No Excuses for Staying the Way You Are

As I said earlier, all of us may have *reasons* why we could harbor ill feelings toward someone. But as caretakers of our own hearts, we have *no excuses* for holding on to those ill feelings.

God's Spirit wants to help you experience the freedom to forgive the person or group of people who offended you. But first, you must recognize that we've all been guilty of offending someone else at some point in our lives. If you stopped and thought for just a few minutes, you'd probably remember a time when you committed the same offense against someone else that has been committed against you. You may be upset about what that person did to you. *But is it possible you are reaping something you have sown?*

> *Before you get angry with the other person, you need to look at yourself and ask if you're experiencing the law of sowing and reaping.*

Before you get angry with the other person, you need to look at yourself and ask if you're experiencing the law of sowing and reaping (*see* Galatians 6:7). It may be difficult to admit that to yourself, but often it's the truth.

When I am tempted to get upset with people who are unfaithful to me in our ministry, the Holy Spirit reminds me of times when I was younger and *I* was unfaithful to those who were over *me*. Remembering my past mistakes helps me overlook and forgive the mistakes of others. It also brings repentance to my heart for the times I have done others wrong with my own actions or lack of actions.

I may have a *reason* to be upset with someone, but I have *no excuse* to stay upset, especially when I remember how much mercy has been shown to me in the past for stupid mistakes and foolish statements I've unintentionally made. *How can anyone who has been shown as much mercy as I have judge others who have made similar mistakes?*

How's Your Memory Working?

We usually become judgmental and unforgiving when we are so focused on what was done to *us* that we forget what we have done to *others* in the past. The truth is, we've probably been guilty in the past of the very offense we're so upset about right now!

We all make mistakes. We all say stupid things we later regret. We all do things, whether right or wrong, that are misunderstood by others. We've all done things that we thought were right at the moment, only to realize later how wrong we were in our actions and attitudes.

Until Christians have their glorified bodies in Heaven, they must deal with their own inconsistencies and blemishes. Even those who spend hours a day in prayer make mistakes that remind them that they are made of dust (*see* Psalm 103:14).

When I deal with staff members who are upset with each other, I remind them of Romans 15:7, which says, "Wherefore receive ye one another, as Christ also received us to the glory of God."

- How did Christ receive you?
  He received you freely — with no strings attached.

- What condition were you in when He saved you?
  You were an ugly mess.

- Have you made any mistakes since you were saved?
  Absolutely yes!

- Have you ever disappointed the Lord since you've been saved?
  Yes, absolutely yes!

- Does Jesus still love you, accept you, and work with you in spite of your hang-ups?
  Thank God, YES!

Romans 15:7 says that this is *exactly* how we are to receive one another. Certainly we must deal with problems when they occur in our relationships. Yes, we must be honest about the things that bother us. But we should never allow an issue to become so big that it separates us from each other.

> *Certainly we must deal with problems when they occur in our relationships. But we should never allow an issue to become so big that it separates us from each other.*

Just consider for a moment all the things *you've* done to the Lord that you'd never tolerate if someone else did them to you. Yet He has never turned from you, and He still patiently works with you all the time.

The devil has been able to destroy many relationships because people refused to be merciful and overlook an offense that they themselves were probably guilty of at an earlier time. *Don't let that describe you.* It is crucial for you to deal with bitterness, resentment, and unforgiveness *before* they get rooted deep down inside your mind and emotions. *Don't allow these attitudes to fester and take root inside you.*

The longer you let bitterness grow in your mind and emotions, the more difficult it will be to uproot and remove. You need to "lay the axe to the root" and *permanently remove* all bitterness before it adversely affects you and your relationship with the person or persons who committed the offense. *Whatever it takes, be a faithful bishop of your own heart!*

> *Whatever it takes, be a faithful bishop of your own heart!*

Think About It

No matter what has been said or done to you, you alone decide how it will ultimately affect you. Something may have happened to victimize you, but you are not a victim. You are in control, and you have the power to choose your response. If you live with the conviction that you are more than a conqueror through Christ, you will refuse to be conquered by another person's attitudes or actions.

Consider the way you've responded in the past to potential offense in your relationships with people. What does your response say about the current state of your relationship with the Lord?

Godly love is the fruit of a strong spirit. A good gauge of how well we have cultivated (or need to cultivate) the fruit of the spirit in our lives is clearly revealed in how we choose to respond during difficult moments with unpleasant people.

Galatians 5:22 (*NIV*) states: "The fruit of the Spirit is love, joy, peace, forbearance, kindness, goodness, faithfulness, gentleness and self-control." Are you short-tempered, impatient, and easily angered with others? In what ways do you recognize your own need to revisit "Fruit of the Spirit 101"? Fruitfulness begins with the decision to act on God's Word — repeatedly and regardless of how you feel.

CHAPTER 7

Uproot Every
'Root of Bitterness'

In order to effectively "lay your axe" to the root of bitterness, you first need to understand how dangerous it is to you and to those around you. Let's take another look at what Hebrews 12:15 says about it: "Looking diligently lest any man fail of the grace of God; lest any root of bitterness springing up trouble you, and thereby many be defiled."

As you recall, the word "root" is the Greek word *pidzo*, which refers to *a root, such as the root of a tree*. These are *roots that have gone down deep and are now deeply embedded*. Therefore, the word *pidzo* often denotes *something that is established or firmly fixed*.

If bitterness against a person becomes *deeply embedded* in your soul, your negative opinion of that person will become *firmly fixed*. As time passes, your thoughts of judgment against him or her will become more developed, rationalized, and established. That root of bitterness will become so firmly fixed inside of you that your angry, judgmental thoughts about the person will actually begin to make sense to you.

When a "root of bitterness" gets this deeply embedded in your mind and emotions, you're no longer just dealing with a "root"; now you have *a mental stronghold*. That stronghold of bitterness will take a lofty position in your mind and emotions. From that position, it will then present a myriad of logical reasons why you shouldn't have anything else to do with that person and why you should keep your distance from him or her.

Again, the word "bitterness" comes from the Greek word *pikria*. It refers to *an inward attitude that is so sour and bitter, it produces a scowl on one's face*. In other words, you become so inwardly *infected* with bitterness that you are outwardly *affected* in your appearance and disposition.

This "bitterness" is acid to one's soul, and eventually it begins to surface. When it does, the fruit it produces is *unkind, caustic, scornful, sarcastic, cynical, mocking, contemptuous,* and *wounding*. Bitterness has nothing good to say about the other person. In fact, it looks for negative things to say about that person to affect others' opinions about him or her as well.

Tell-Tale Signs That Bitterness Is Growing in Your Life

When you find yourself constantly saying something derogatory about someone else, pay attention to what's happening. What you're saying about that person is a tell-tale sign that some bad seed is trying to take root in your heart.

Let's go back to the picture painted by the words of Hebrews 12:15, which helps us recognize when bad seed is beginning to produce destructive fruit in our lives. It says, "...lest any root of bitterness *springing up* trouble you...." The words "springing up" are from the Greek word *phuoo*, which depicts *a tiny, tender plant that is just starting to sprout and grow.* It isn't a large plant yet; rather, it's a small seedling that is just beginning to pierce through the soil. However, the very fact that it's peeking through the soil means there is a seed hidden in the soil producing this new plant. The writer of Hebrews is telling us that it's our responsibility to pay attention to our hearts, our attitudes, and our words so we can recognize and remove every bitter sprig before it becomes deeply rooted and springs up to blossom with deadly, poisonous fruit.

This is a very significant picture. It tells us that bitterness doesn't overwhelm us all at once. Instead, it grows a little here

> *Bitterness doesn't overwhelm us all at once. Instead, it grows a little here and a little there until it finally becomes a huge, ugly growth that defiles our entire lives.*

and a little there until it finally becomes a huge, ugly growth that defiles our entire lives.

Bitterness usually starts peeking up out of the depths of our souls in the form of negative thoughts about another person or a sour, sharp, distrusting, cynical attitude toward someone. If the root is not quickly uprooted and removed, that bitterness will eventually become a full-blown tree that produces *bitter*, *wounding*, *hurtful*, and *scornful* fruit for everyone who eats of it.

As bad as this fruit is for others, it hurts no one more than it does you. Think for a moment about the woman I told you about earlier who lives in an emotional prison of unforgiveness. The people she despises have moved on with their lives, but she has remained *paralyzed* and *dysfunctional* behind those walls of offense and resentment.

Hebrews 12:15 shouts its warning: If you don't stop these attitudes, they will eventually "trouble" you. That word "trouble" is from the Greek word *enochleo*, which means *to trouble, harass, vex, annoy*, or *stalk*. It refers to *something inside that bothers and upsets you so much, you are constantly pestered by thoughts about it*. In fact, your whole life is *stalked* by these *hassling, tormenting thoughts*. What you allowed to take root and fester inside your soul has now become *a major nuisance* to your peace that keeps you upset and emotionally torn up all the time.

This word makes sense when you think about the times you've been offended in your life. Isn't it true that you're usually more affected by the situation than the one who offended you?

In fact, the offender often doesn't even know he's offended you! That person probably didn't wake up that morning and think, *I'm going to see how many people I can offend today!* Most offenses are accidental, so the offender may not even know he offended you.

But when you're the one who is offended, you can be hounded by what happened. Furthermore, the thought that can really stalk you is that the person who offended you seems so carefree and unaffected by the incident, as though he's not even concerned about what he did to you! Meanwhile, you still go through life feeling hounded, harassed, and stalked by what that person said or did.

So take a moment to examine your heart:

- Do you have a grudge against someone that just gnaws away at you all the time?

- Every time you see that person, do you feel something sharp and ugly inside?

- When you hear about that person being blessed, do you wonder how God could possibly do that when he or she did such an ugly thing to you?

- Do negative thoughts like these pester and bother you all the time?

> *Take a moment to examine your heart: Do you have a grudge against someone that just gnaws away at you all the time?*

If you relate to the situation I just described, watch out! Bitterness, resentment, and unforgiveness are now *hounding* and *stalking* you! These foul attitudes are tormenting you more than they are anyone else.

The very thought of the person who offended you *troubles* and *harasses* you. You're annoyed every time you see that person. You even get upset if the Lord blesses him or uses him in a way to bless others. Yet that person is probably unaffected by your inward struggle. Instead, he is probably moving on in life while you wallow in unforgiveness! If this sounds familiar, then Hebrews 12:15 may be describing *you* when it says, "…lest any root of bitterness springing up trouble you…."

Bitterness left unchecked will begin to take root and thrust its shoots deep inside your heart. Its sharp, caustic poison will continue to trouble, irritate, and vex you until you finally deal with the bitterness you've harbored in your heart. If you don't get a grip on yourself right now and let the Holy Spirit help you permanently put these feelings aside, you'll fulfill the next part of the verse as well that says, "…and many be *defiled*."

Be Careful What You Dump on People Who Are Listening to You!

The word "defiled" is from the Greek word *miaini* and it means *to spill, to spot,* or *to stain*. It carries the idea of *a permanent reminder of a past action or a past deed done*. An example of this word is what would happen if you walked across someone's white carpet carrying a glass of grape juice and then tripped and fell, spilling grape juice all over the carpet. You might scrub and scrub and *scrub*, but there would still be a stain there — a permanent reminder of what you did.

What a powerful picture this is for you and me! It tells us that when we begin to "run at the mouth" and say bad things about someone else, we have a devastating effect on the listeners' attitudes. As our root of bitterness rages out of control, our derogatory words *taint*, *spot*, *soil*, and *ruin* the way our listeners perceive the person we're talking about. Previously they may have held a high opinion of the person we're talking about. But by the time we're finished ranting and raving and expressing our bitterness (which may be dressed in a variety of disguises), we have completely soured their opinion of that person. They have been *soiled* by what we *dumped* on them.

> **When we begin to "run at the mouth" and say bad things about someone else, we have a devastating effect on the listeners' attitudes.**

An example would be a father who has always loved his church — until something happens in the church that offends him. Rather than release the offense and forgive, he goes home and *fumes* about what happened. The longer he fumes about it, the angrier he gets. As his anger grows, he starts venting and talking about what he thinks and feels. He is so *upset* with that church!

Before this moment, this man's children loved their church. They *thought* their father loved it too. But day after day, they listen to him rage about how bad the pastor is or how badly he has been treated. This father doesn't realize that his words are defiling his children.

Soon *the children* begin to feel what *their father* feels. They see what *he* sees and believe what *he* believes. It isn't too long before they are carrying the same bitter feelings toward the church as their father — even though nothing wrong has ever been done to them!

The minds and hearts of these children have been *tainted*, *stained*, and *spotted* by a father who should have kept his mouth shut, gone to the Cross, and allowed the Spirit of God to liberate him from those bitter emotions. Instead, he dumped his bitterness on his family. Now he's not the only one who has an attitude problem; he has imparted his bad attitude to his children as well. And if his children have a negative attitude toward the church when they grow up, much of the blame will be laid at that father's feet for not keeping his mouth shut and being more mature.

Have you ever been guilty of relating to another person something negative that someone said or did to you? If you have, you defiled the person you talked to in the process, staining his thoughts with a corrupt opinion that will change how he sees and responds to the one who offended you. Every time he sees your offender, he'll remember that report you gave. This is precisely how gossip-fueled scandals are created, many of which cause damage that is sometimes irrevocable. No one wins when bitterness is allowed to take root and then spring up to defile many.

If you internalize an offense and then refuse to deal with it, you trip up your forward progress in life. Your heart begins to harden, and you become less and less guarded with your words about the offender because out of the abundance of the heart, the mouth speaks. Sadly, every time you speak about your offense, releasing words steeped in bitterness and animosity, you stain the ears of your listeners. The offense, once limited to and contained in your heart alone, is released to spread and contaminate the hearts of others, leaving a sour reminder of the destruction unchecked bitterness can cause.

It's just a fact that when a root of bitterness is not *uprooted* and *removed* by God's Spirit, it doesn't just adversely affect you — it affects a lot of other people as well. Ultimately, it has the power to affect every friend or relative in your life.

> *When a root of bitterness is not UPROOTED and REMOVED by God's Spirit, it doesn't just adversely affect you — it affects a lot of other people as well.*

What a pity it is to dump all your negative garbage on your friends and loved ones, defiling them with a spiritual problem that may hound them for years. It would be far better for you to go to the Cross and deal with it as a mature person than to sow a lot of bad seed that you'll only end up reaping later!

I can emphatically say this from personal experience. In the case of that one brother who committed so many wrongs against me and my ministry, I finally learned to keep my heart free of bitterness. Although it wasn't an overnight process, a time came when I could say that I had truly let it all go and moved on. The alternative would have been disastrous not only to me, but also to my family and ministry. If the bitterness that polluted my heart had been left unchecked, its poisonous influence would have extended beyond me to infect and defile many others. I'm so thankful I found God's way out of the trap of offense!

You WILL Have an Opportunity To Get Offended!

In Luke 17:1, Jesus said, "...It is impossible but that offences will come...." The word "offense" is from the Greek word *skandalos*, from which we get the word *scandal*. This word refers to something that causes you *to trip*, *to fall*, or *to stumble*. It has been translated as *a stumbling block* or *a stumbling stone*.

But in plainer language, what is an *offense*? An offense occurs when you see, hear, or experience a behavior that is so different from what you expected that it causes you to *falter*, *totter*, and *wobble* in your soul and leaves you *reeling* on the inside. In fact, you just about *lose your footing* when this event occurs because it takes you so off guard. Now your opinion of that person you once admired has become adversely affected.

We've all experienced this kind of disappointment at some point in our lives. As long as we live and breathe, we must combat offense and *refuse* to allow it to have a place in our hearts and minds.

Even worse, we've all been the *source* of offense at one point or another. The offense may have been unintentional on our part. We may not have even known we offended anyone until the person came and informed us that he or she was upset. But regardless of our intent, someone became offended by something we did or didn't do.

> *As long as we live and breathe, we must combat offense and REFUSE to allow it to have a place in our hearts and minds.*

- Have you ever offended someone?

- When you found out about it, were you shocked?

- When the news finally reached you that you had offended that person, were you surprised to hear how he or she perceived what you did or said?

This happens to everyone. Through the years, I've learned to do the best I can to avoid being a source of offense to anyone.

At the same time, I try not to be too shocked if I find out that someone, somewhere, has gotten offended.

Because people come from different backgrounds, wake up in different moods, and go through a host of different experiences in their lives, their interpretation of your actions and words may frequently be very different than what you intended. You can be almost 99 percent certain that someone along the way will misinterpret something you do or say.

So often the hidden root of wars, family divisions, broken friendships, dissolved marriages, divided churches, and so on, can be found in the tangled mess of:

- Misperceptions

- Misunderstandings

- Misinterpretations

- Mistaken motives

As Christians, we must do everything in our power to communicate correct messages to one another. And whenever misunderstanding does result in offense between ourselves and others, we must do everything in our power to bring healing and forgiveness.

If you discover that you've been a source of offense to someone, take the mature path and go ask for forgiveness, even if you think you weren't wrong in the first place. Don't get defensive; that only makes the problem worse and often leads to an argument. Do everything you can to bury that offense and destroy what the devil is trying to do. Make it your personal aim to help that other person overcome what he or she *thinks* you did or said. Helping the other person attain a position of peace is more important than proving who is right or wrong.

If you discover that you've been a source of offense to someone, take the mature path and go ask for forgiveness, even if you think you weren't wrong in the first place.

What if You Are the Offended One?

In Chapter Two, we discussed Jesus' instructions to us if we become offended. His words are found in Luke 17:3,4: "…If thy brother trespass against thee, rebuke him; and if he repent, forgive him. And if he trespass against thee seven times in a day, and seven times in a day turn again to thee, saying, I repent; thou shalt forgive him."

Walking in forgiveness is part of your lifestyle as a mature believer.

Jesus taught that if someone wrongs you in some way, *you are to go talk to the person about it*. If the person apologizes and repents of his or her actions, *you are to forgive that person and let go of the offense*. If it's difficult for you to do that, you need to go to the Cross and ask the Holy Spirit to help you do it.

Walking in forgiveness is part of your lifestyle as a mature believer. Besides, hasn't the Lord forgiven you many times for sins you have committed against Him? How often has He forgiven you for doing the same thing again and again? If you've *received* this kind of mercy, isn't it right that you should *give* the same mercy to others?

When the disciples heard Jesus' teaching about forgiveness, they said to the Lord, "...Increase our faith" (Luke 17:5). That was the equivalent of saying, *"Lord, what You've just asked us to do is very hard! You have to increase our faith and help us believe we can forgive so many times!"*

The truth is, God has already given you all the faith you need to forgive others when they offend or hurt you, whether or not they ever apologize or seek reconciliation themselves. But you still have to make the decision to *use* that faith to pull out every root of bitterness while it's still a little seedling. Don't wait to "lay the axe to the root" until you have a huge tree of anger and bitterness defiling your life!

Think About It

The fruit of righteousness is produced when you think on, act on, and speak in agreement with the Word of God, allowing it to fertilize the soil of your heart. The nature of the root you are feeding with your thoughts and deeds will determine the quality of fruit you'll see in your life.

How often do you think about the person or the situation that offended you? How frequently does this offense work its way into your conversations? Do you trust God to work all things together for your good in this matter, or are you hoping to eventually get revenge in some way?

"Work at living in peace with everyone.... Watch out that no poisonous root of bitterness grows up to trouble you, corrupting many" (Hebrews 12:14,15 *NLT*). Seeking peace doesn't always mean the restoration of a relationship, since more than one person's free will is involved. But it does mean the removal of strife. Wounded people wound other people if they don't take action and make a decision to avoid that trap.

What steps do you need to take to allow God to heal your heart from the wounds caused by others in your life? What must you do to remove strife and ensure peace so that you can live free from troubling emotions and those around you won't be adversely affected?

It's Time for You To Let It Go!

*I*t's difficult for most people to confront someone else regarding an offense, but sometimes confrontation is necessary. In fact, avoiding confrontation is often what causes bad feelings to turn inward and fester into something much worse. Those ugly feelings can sit in the pit of a person's stomach, churning and churning away, until he becomes so upset that he can hardly think about anything else.

> *Avoiding confrontation is often what causes bad feelings to turn inward and fester into something much worse.*

Usually it's better to kindly say what you feel and get over it than to let those raw emotions turn into an ugly monster, waiting to crawl out at an opportune moment and attack its victim. That is frequently what happens when you allow negative emotions to fester unchecked. Confrontation may be uneasy and uncomfortable for you to do. However, it's a lot less painful than having to apologize later for erupting in a fit of flesh just like a volcano that spews destructive lava all over its surroundings.

This is exactly why Jesus said, "...If thy brother trespass against thee, rebuke him; and if he repent, forgive him" (Luke 17:3). Remember, the word "trespass" means *to violate a rule, to cross a line,* or *to commit a grievance.* Jesus was saying that if you believe someone has violated you, crossed a line he shouldn't have crossed, or committed what you perceive to be a grievance against you, you need to "rebuke" that person for what he did. The word "rebuke" doesn't mean you should speak harshly to him. It means you need to directly and honestly confront him about the matter.

This issue of honesty is a big one in the Body of Christ. Many believers are dishonest about what they really think and feel. Inside they are livid with anger toward someone about a perceived offense; yet they smile at that person and pretend like everything is all right when it isn't at all. This dishonesty secretly divides believers and keeps God's power from freely flowing between members of the Body of Christ.

According to the apostle Paul, the ability to "speak the truth in love" is one of the marks of a mature believer (Ephesians

4:15). I realize we may enjoy measuring our spirituality by how well we prophesy or speak in tongues, but that is not the mark of maturity Paul gives us. Relationships are the bottom line in life. How well we fare in our relationships with others tells the real story of how mature we are in the Lord.

> *How well we fare in our relationships with others tells the real story of how mature we are in the Lord.*

Many believers have hidden disagreements or secret, petty grievances against other people, yet they go around smiling and acting as if everything is all right. These people are not just being dishonest — they're engaging in outright *lying* and *deception*.

When you refuse to be honest about your feelings and confront an offense, you're just as wrong as the one who violated your rights and stepped over the line. Until you're willing to be honest and "speak the truth in love," you have no right to judge anyone else.

Remember, Jesus said, "...If thy brother trespass against thee, *rebuke him*..." (Luke 17:3). That means if you are going to be mature in your relationships, you must learn how to confront others when you feel they've wronged you. It may be hard to do, but it's a lot less painful and leaves less scars than living with a heart and soul filled with bitterness and resentment.

How To Confront Someone

When you have to confront someone regarding an offense that you perceive he has committed against you, I recommend that you take the following three steps:

STEP #1:

Don't confront anyone until you've first made it a matter of prayer.

Prayer resolves a lot of problems by itself. There have been times in my own life when I've been upset with someone, only to discover after getting into the presence of God and praying about the matter that my attitude was uglier than that of the one who wronged me. Once I recognized my own condition, I couldn't hold a thing against the other person anymore; I just wanted to get my own heart right before God.

Prayer will put you in a position where God can speak to your own heart. After praying, if you still sense that you are supposed to confront the other person, pray for that person first. The Spirit of God may give you a strategy regarding what to say, as well as when and how to say it.

Believe me, it's crucial that you receive directions from the Holy Spirit about how to talk to someone regarding an offense. To confront a person without praying about it first is to barge into the middle of the fray ill-equipped and unprepared. Therefore, let prayer be a time of spiritual fine-tuning and preparation to do what you need to do. As you pray, spend a few minutes thanking God for your offender. This will help bring you to a new level so you can deal with the issue at hand in the right spirit.

Remember the good things that person has done. Take time to reflect on all the good moments you've had with him or her and all the benefits you've gained in life as a result of that relationship. It's difficult to remain angry at someone when you're thanking God for that person at the same time!

To confront a person without praying about it first is to barge into the middle of the fray ill-equipped and unprepared.

Step #2:

Don't confront anyone with a judgmental attitude.

We've all made mistakes — *and that includes you*! So assume that your offender would *not* deliberately hurt or offend you. Take a positive position about the other person.

When you do finally sit down to talk with the person who offended you, start the conversation by assuring him that you're sure he didn't intend to do what he did. Tell him that the devil somehow got into the middle of your relationship with him through his actions — and that now you want to get the enemy back *out* of the relationship as you get your heart right with him. This immediately removes any sense of an accusatory spirit and puts the spotlight on the devil instead of on that person. The issues will still be dealt with, but from a different perspective.

> *The purpose of this time of confrontation is not to prove how wrong the other person is. It's to learn how to work together better and how to keep the channel of communication open and in the light.*

Starting from this approach is much more beneficial than taking a defensive approach that treats the other person as if he were your adversary. Remember, that person is not your enemy; he isn't on the other side of the line, fighting a battle against you. Your relationship may be going through some rough times right now, but you still need to view the two of you as being on the same side. The purpose of this time of confrontation is not to prove how wrong the other person is. It's to learn how to work together better and how to keep the channel of communication open and in the light.

STEP #3:

Remember that you, too, have been offensive in the past.

Never forget that you've more than likely offended people in the past. You probably didn't intend to do it. You may not have even known you did it until the person later told you. You were probably embarrassed or sad when you heard how the devil had used something you said or did to leave a wrong impression. You knew that your intentions were not to hurt.

When you were in this type of situation, didn't you want the person you had offended to tell you the truth rather than to walk around harboring bad feelings about you? Weren't you glad when that lie of the devil was exposed and your relationship was made right again? Weren't you thankful for the opportunity to put things right with that other person?

So when someone offends you, remember that you've stood in his or her shoes in the past. Were you forgiven at that time? Were you shown mercy? Now it's time for you to show the same forgiveness and mercy to someone else that was shown to you in the past.

> *It's time for you to show the same forgiveness and mercy to someone else that was shown to you in the past.*

If you still feel the need to confront the person who offended you after following these three steps, you should now be able to do it with the right attitude. You have spent time in God's presence and prayed about the matter. Now your heart is free, liberated from negative feelings and attitudes toward that person. You're finally in a position to go to him or her in a spirit of love and reconciliation instead of in a spirit of accusation. As Jesus said, "...if he repent, *forgive* him" (Luke 17:3).

Let It Go

Let's review what that word "forgive" means. It's the Greek word *aphiemi*, which means *to permanently dismiss*, *to liberate completely, to discharge, to send away,* or *to release*. It was used in a secular sense in New Testament times to mean *to cancel a debt* or *to release someone from an obligation of a contract, a commitment, or a promise*. Thus, it means to *forfeit any right to hold a person captive to a previous commitment or a wrong he has committed*.

In essence, the word "forgive" — the Greek word *aphiemi* — is the picture of totally *freeing* and *releasing* someone. As I said earlier, I like the modern paraphrase of this Greek word: No matter what the offense is, we need to *let it go*.

> *You and I don't have the privilege of holding people hostage to their past actions if they repent and ask us to forgive them.*

Let's look at Luke 17:3 one more time: "Take heed to yourselves: If thy brother trespass against thee, rebuke him; and if he repent, forgive him." That means you and I don't have the privilege of holding people hostage to their past actions if they repent and ask us to forgive them. If they sincerely seek forgiveness for offending us, we are obligated to "let it go."

It's amazing how cheated our flesh feels when someone quickly repents for the hurt he has caused us. You see, our flesh enjoys holding someone's grievance over his head and making him pay for what he did — even if it's just for a little while.

But if your offender repents and sincerely asks for forgiveness, Jesus said you are to *forgive* him. In other words, you must put away the offense and no longer hold on to it. You must release those ugly feelings you've held against that person. *You have to let it go.* I guarantee you, that's when you find out how mature you really are!

So are you able to let go of that offense? Are you able to put it away and to stop dragging it up again and again?

Exercising true forgiveness means that you can no longer hold the grievance against that person. Just as God removed your sin as far as the east is from the west (*see* Psalm 103:12), now you must decide that this person is *freed* in regard to that past offense. Once you forgive your offender, you can't drag up the offense again and again. You have released him completely; now he is freed, released, and liberated from that sin. *You never have the right or privilege to pull out that offense later and use it against him. It is GONE!*

That person is so freed from his offense against you that it can never be an issue again — at least it can't be as long as he doesn't repeat the same offense. You have no choice but to *let it go*!

Taking It to the Next Level

As if this wasn't already hard enough to hear, Jesus took His teaching about forgiveness to the next level in Luke 17:4, saying, "And if he trespass against thee seven times in a day, and seven times in a day turn again to thee, saying, I repent; thou shalt forgive him."

Forgiving a person who truly offended you can be a challenge. But let's say you finally work up the nerve to confront that person. You decide to forgive him and release him from the sin he committed against you. A week goes by — and then he does it *again*!

Now what are you going to do?

Jesus said if someone trespasses against you *seven times* in one day and then turns to you seven times to sincerely ask you to forgive him, you are to *forgive* him. In other words, as long as that person is willing to confess that he was wrong and is sincerely trying to change, you are to be mature enough to keep forgiving and to *let it go*! That's why the disciples answered, "Lord, increase our faith!" (*see* Luke 17:5).

Forgiving someone once is one thing, but Jesus said that He expects us to keep forgiving that person over and over again! The flesh says, "Come on, give me a break! How many times am I supposed to forgive? Does God expect me to just keep forgiving that person again and again and again?"

Well, look at verse 4 again. Jesus plainly taught that as long as the person tries to change — as long as he or she keeps trying to repent — you and I are to keep forgiving, even if it means we have to do it seven times in a single day! No wonder the disciples basically said, *"Wow, Lord, if we're going to live at that high level of forgiveness, You have to increase our faith! We don't know if we have enough faith to live like that!"*

And as we saw before, Jesus didn't stop there. He took this issue of forgiveness *even further* when He said in Mark 11:25 (*NKJV*), "And whenever you stand praying, if you have *anything* against *anyone*, forgive him, that your Father in heaven may also forgive you your trespasses." *God has simply given us no room for excuses when it comes to letting go of offense!*

Jesus' next words to the disciples in Luke 17:6 were very significant. He said, "If ye had faith as a grain of mustard seed, ye might say unto this sycamine tree, Be thou plucked up by the root, and be thou planted in the sea; and it should obey you." In the next chapter, I'm going to show you just how much Jesus' response reveals to us about this subject of unforgiveness.

Think About It

"Instead be kind to each other, tenderhearted, forgiving one another, just as God through Christ has forgiven you" (Ephesians 4:32 *NLT*). When you view your own behavior in the light of this verse, how do you measure up? What do you need to work on? What relationships do you tend to take for granted, treating them with less kindness and respect than you do those whom you seek to impress?

Letting go of a grievance on one occasion can be difficult enough. But how have you responded when you have to forgive the same person for the same offense again and again? What offensive words or behavior have *you* needed to be forgiven of repeatedly?

Why Jesus Compared Unforgiveness to the Sycamine Tree

*I*n Luke 17:6, Jesus gave an extremely vivid picture of the evil effects of unforgiveness. He also told the disciples how to get rid of unforgiveness in this verse.

Jesus said, "…If ye had faith as a grain of mustard seed, ye might say unto this sycamine tree, Be thou plucked up by the root, and be thou planted in the sea; and it should obey you." Notice that He likened the *unforgiveness* He talked about in verses 1-5 to a *sycamine tree*. Before we discuss how to uproot unforgiveness, let's first see why Jesus used the sycamine tree in this illustration. Why didn't He use a plum tree, apple tree, or orange tree? *Was there a particular reason He used the sycamine tree to symbolize unforgiveness?*

Important Facts
About the Sycamine Tree

Consider these facts about the sycamine tree, and you will understand why Jesus used it as a symbol of unforgiveness. There is no doubt that Jesus chose the sycamine tree because of the following facts:

FACT #1:

In Egypt and the Middle East, the sycamine tree was the preferred wood for building caskets.

Caskets! Just think of it — the tree that was most commonly used to make caskets is the example Jesus used to depict bitterness, resentment, and unforgiveness!

The sycamine tree was the preferred wood for building coffins because it possessed these characteristics:

- It grew quickly. (This was beneficial because people needed large amounts of the wood for making coffins.)

- It grew in many different kinds of environments (making it easily accessible).

- It grew best in dry conditions (making it easy to grow even in bad conditions).

- Its wood was very durable (a desired quality for the making of coffins).

One look at this list, and I understand why Jesus likened the sycamine tree to unforgiveness. Just like the sycamine tree:

- *Unforgiveness grows very quickly.*
  It doesn't take long at all for unforgiveness to get out of control, growing so large that it starts taking over the place where it's planted — in this case, *your heart!*

- *Unforgiveness grows in every environment.*
  It doesn't matter where a person is from, where he lives, what his culture is like, or what level of society he belongs to — unforgiveness grows in human hearts everywhere. It's *universal.*

- *Unforgiveness grows best in dry conditions.*
  Unforgiveness thrives where spiritually dry conditions exist. Where there is no repentance, no joy, no fruit of the Spirit — that's where unforgiveness grows and flourishes.

  > *Unforgiveness thrives where spiritually dry conditions exist. Where there is no repentance, no joy, no fruit of the Spirit — that's where unforgiveness grows and flourishes.*

- *Unforgiveness will bury you.*
  The fact that the sycamine tree was used for building caskets tells us that unforgiveness will bury us more quickly than anything else! Unforgiveness is used by Satan to put us six feet under the ground.

It not only works death in our physical bodies, but it also kills our spiritual life and makes us spiritually lifeless.

FACT #2:

The sycamine tree has a very large and deep root structure.

The sycamine tree has one of the deepest root structures of all the trees in the Middle East. It is a robust tree that grows to a height of thirty feet or more.

The sycamine tree is very hard to kill because its roots go down so *deep*. Even cutting the tree down to its base doesn't guarantee its death because the roots, hidden deep under the ground, keep forcing their way to the surface to produce new life again and again.

> *Unforgiveness must be dealt with clear down to the roots. Otherwise, it will keep springing up again and again.*

No wonder Jesus used this tree as an example of *unforgiveness!*

Like the sycamine tree, unforgiveness must be dealt with clear down to the roots. Otherwise, it will keep springing up again and again. Its roots go down deep into the human soul, and only *genuine repentance* can rip those roots out so they will stop growing back over and over again.

Fact #3:

The sycamine tree produces fruit that is bitter to eat.

The sycamine tree and fig tree are very similar in appearance. The fruit these two trees produce even looks identical; however, the fruit of the sycamine tree is extremely bitter. The fruit of the sycamine looks just as delicious as a fig — but when tasted, it's very bitter and unpleasant.

Figs were expensive in New Testament times, so poorer people ate the fruit of the sycamine tree as a substitute for the fig. However, the sycamine fruit was so bitter, it couldn't be eaten whole. It had to be *nibbled on* a little bit at a time. After a pause, the eater could start nibbling again, but a person could never devour a whole piece of this fruit at one time. It was just too *tart* and *pungent* to eat at one sitting

Like the sycamine fruit, unforgiveness is *bitter, sharply tart,* and *pungent.* Most people "chew" on their feelings of bitterness and unforgiveness for a long time. They nibble on the offense for a while; then they pause to digest what they've eaten. Then they start nibbling on it again — taking one little bite, then another and another.

As these people think and meditate on the perceived offense, they internalize their bitter feelings toward the person or persons who offended them. In the end, the sour, bitter fruit of unforgiveness makes *them* sour and bitter as well.

Also, just as poorer people were the ones who ate the sycamine fruit, those who sit around and constantly meditate on all the wrongs committed against them are usually bound up in all kinds of poverty as well. Certainly these people become *spiritually poor* as they constantly chew on that bitter fruit. But they are also frequently *defeated, depressed, sick,* and *financially poor*.

FACT #4:

The sycamine tree is pollinated by wasps.

The sycamine tree is pollinated when a wasp sticks its stinger right into the heart of the fruit. Since the wasp's sting initiates the pollination process, the sycamine tree and its fruit could not be reproduced without it.

This makes me think of all the times I've heard people say: "I'm sorry, but I've been stung by that person once, and I'm not going to be stung again! What he did hurt me so badly that I'd be a fool to let him get close enough to sting me again!"

Is it possible that these people were "stung" by a situation specially designed by the devil to pollinate their hearts and souls with unforgiveness? *Did Satan's "wasp" get to them?*

If you keep your heart free of offense, the devil *cannot* produce this foul fruit inside you. The best way to avoid the destructive effects of unforgiveness in your life is to determine that you will *never be offended* in the first place! If you'll keep the stinger of that wasp out of your heart, you'll never have to uproot a huge tree of bitterness later!

It's obvious why Jesus used the sycamine tree in this illustration regarding unforgiveness. Bitterness provides Satan with a perfect "coffin" in which to bury the effectiveness of your spiritual life. Its roots grow quickly and penetrate deeply to take over your mind, your emotions — indeed, every area of your life. Finally, the bitter fruit it produces is an ideal snack to "chew" on if you choose to hold on to offense and remain in spiritual and material poverty.

> *Bitterness provides Satan with a perfect "coffin" in which to bury the effectiveness of your spiritual life.*

But now that the problem has been identified and you better understand the seriousness of the issue, what can you do to get rid of bitterness, resentment, and unforgiveness in your life?

It's Time To *Uproot* and *Remove* That Tree!

Jesus used the illustration of the sycamine tree to tell us how to uproot and remove offenses and unforgiveness from the heart. In Luke 17:6, He gave us the secret weapon that can enable us to jerk those roots clear out of the ground of our hearts and send them to a place where they will *never* reproduce in us again.

Jesus said, "…If ye had faith as a grain of mustard seed, ye might *say* unto this sycamine tree, Be thou plucked up by the root, and be thou planted in the sea; and it should obey you." Notice He said, "…ye might *say* unto this sycamine tree.…" In order to get rid of bitterness and unforgiveness, you have to rise up and *speak* to those destructive devices. Take authority over them in Jesus' name with the words of your mouth!

> *In order to get rid of bitterness and unforgiveness, you have to rise up and speak to those destructive devices. Take authority over them in Jesus' name with the words of your mouth!*

Don't wait until you feel like doing it because I promise you — you never will. If you depend on your feelings and emotions, you'll never be free of offense and unforgiveness. Your feelings and emotions will tell you that you have a right and a very good reason to feel the way you do. Therefore, you must make the choice to turn off your emotions and think with a sound mind!

It's time for you to accept personal responsibility for this inward condition. Quit blaming everyone else for all your bad attitudes, and acknowledge that something *inside you* needs to be removed. Jesus said you must *speak* to that "sycamine tree" and tell it to *go*!

- If you don't speak to your emotions, they will speak to you.

- If you don't take authority over your emotions, they will take authority over you.

- If you don't rise up and conquer those feelings of bitterness and unforgiveness, they will rise up and conquer you.

- Quit letting your emotions tell you what to think, what to do, and how to react.

- It's time for you to do the talking and take command of your thought life!

You have to speak to bitterness, resentment, and unforgiveness as *enemies* that have come to corrupt your soul. You must make a firm decision not to tolerate this spiritual pestilence in your thought life — not even for a second. And, if necessary, you must speak to unforgiveness *again, again, and again* — until it is finally *uprooted* and *removed* forever.

You have to go for the roots! If you want to be free, it's going to take an attitude that says, *"I'm going to grab on to the roots of this poisonous growth and yank it clear out of my soul — and I'm not going to stop until I'm totally free!"*

Command Those Attitudes
To Be Planted in the Sea!

Salt water won't allow a plant to grow; the salt will kill it. Therefore, once a plant or tree is thrown into seawater, it becomes a *dead issue*. It doesn't matter how hard you try to make that plant grow again, it will never happen. Its life is gone forever!

That is precisely how you have to deal with those dead issues you've spoken to and commanded to *be removed* from your life. Once you've told them to *go*, don't allow them to reestablish their roots again. They are dead issues — and they are to remain dead forever.

If your flesh calls out to you, luring you to go over all those old hurts again, don't allow that bitter tree to come back to life again. Throw it into the sea of forgetfulness! Bury it in the sea so deeply that its roots can *never again* regain a foothold in your soul.

> *If your flesh calls out to you, luring you to go over all those old hurts again, don't allow that bitter tree to come back to life again. Throw it into the sea of forgetfulness!*

Jesus instructed us to say to the sycamine tree, "...Be thou plucked up by the root, and be thou planted in the sea...." Notice what He says next: "...and it should obey you." The word "obey" is the Greek word *hupakouo*, which means *to submit to* or *to obey*.

Your out-of-control emotions behave just like an out-of-control child. They will rant, rave, and carry on all day long — *until* you finally stand up and tell them to straighten up and act right!

Flesh will pout, throw a temper tantrum, and carry on to a ridiculous extent until you decide that *enough is enough*. When you finally make the choice to rise up, speak to your emotions, and exert your authority in Jesus Christ, *your flesh will obey your commands*!

- If you don't take authority over your emotions and flesh, they will continue to dominate and hound you.

- If you'll stand up to your destructive emotions and plant them in the sea forever, they will obey you, and you will be free!

So refuse to allow your flesh to be your master. Let the Spirit of God inside you take charge and start calling the shots. Bitterness and unforgiveness have absolutely no place in your life, so *uproot* and *remove* them once and for all!

Think About It

Harboring unforgiveness toward another person injects quick-acting poison directly into the main arteries of your own soul and body.

Do you find it difficult to maintain your spiritual strength, peace of mind, and physical health? Think back on instances of your own past carnal outbursts. Were they followed by bouts of spiritual lethargy or bodily weakness? Where have you allowed bitterness to fester and serve as host to parasitic issues of trouble or lack?

Your flesh is not your friend. It is easily enticed to agree with the devil, inciting your emotions to yield to anger, resentment, and strife.

In what situations have you allowed your emotions to usurp authority over your spirit and gain dominance over your thoughts and actions? What are the warning signs that let you know your emotions are luring you into a conflict? What can you do next time you're in this type of situation to take control over your heated emotions and avoid reacting to or creating an offense?

Ten Practical Suggestions To Keep Your Heart Free of Bitterness and Strife

*I*t's a fact that none of us can escape. From time to time, situations arise in all of our lives that entice us to get *upset, offended,* or *resentful.* These situations are usually over minor issues that get blown out of proportion. But by the time we realize how petty the issues are, it's often too late. Bad words have already been spoken, and hurt is lodged deep in the soul. The only thing left to do is to begin the process of getting over the hurt and offense. However, this is a much more difficult thing to do than to just deal with the situation differently in the first place.

Because this is a predicament that everyone faces at one time or another, I've written ten suggestions that I've learned to apply in my own life to help keep my emotions in balance and my heart free of offense. These practical suggestions may not seem deep or profound. But if they help keep your heart free of strife and offense, they are *mighty* and *powerful*!

Read the following points carefully. I believe they will help you keep the door closed to the devil so he can't destroy your relationship with the people you love, the people you work with, or those with whom you serve the Lord.

Suggestion #1:

If you think you're getting in strife, ask to be excused for a few minutes.

> *Devil strikes our minds and emotions when we are physically or emotionally exhausted. He knows that when we're tired, it's harder to hear and see things correctly.*

I've learned that when I'm weak and tired, I'm more susceptible to an attack from the devil. It's amazing how many times the devil strikes our minds and emotions when we are physically or emotionally exhausted. He knows that when we're tired, it's harder to hear and see things correctly.

For instance, have you ever gotten so deeply involved in a conversation that you couldn't see your way out? I have. The longer you talk, the more trapped you feel.

Even worse, you can't even remember how the tangled-up conversation got started in the first place! You're exhausted from trying to prove your point or understand the other person's view. Instead of sensing the sweet fruit of the Spirit flowing from your heart, you feel like you're about to erupt in a fit of raging carnality and say things you'll later regret.

When you find yourself in this type of situation, ask to be excused for a few minutes. Give yourself an opportunity to get a grip on your emotions and see things in a new light. You may be tempted to get into strife just because you are physically or mentally tired. That weariness may be affecting you so you can't accurately hear or understand what the other person is trying to communicate to you.

At times I become involved in a situation in which stress and strife begin to develop between me and someone I love or whose cooperation I need. If I'm tired when this happens, my perception is more easily distorted. As the conversation gets more and more intense, I sometimes feel like I'm losing track of the point we are both trying to make. Frustrations arise. Conflict erupts. I later end up regretting that I didn't put on the brakes and stop making such a big deal over something so insignificant.

That's why I've learned the wisdom of walking away from this type of situation for a short break. When I realize my emotions are getting bent out of shape about something that really shouldn't be a big deal, I just ask for a few minutes to be by myself.

Satan loves to attack people when they are tired. So instead of letting him take advantage of you when you're weak and tired, be smart. Tell the other party or parties involved in the potential conflict that you need to take a break for a little while. Go enjoy a walk around the block, pray, or read your Bible. Do something that takes your mind off the issue at hand and helps you relax for just a little while before you have to come back to deal with that issue.

I'll tell you a secret I learned years ago that has helped me avoid strife in my own life. When I'm tempted to get upset with someone, I look for the opportunity to just get away, close my eyes, and sleep for fifteen minutes. When I'm able to do that, I often awaken with a brand-new approach and a positive attitude toward the problem I'm facing. Although that problem may have seemed overwhelming to me just a short time before, my little nap clears my mind and helps me get started again with a healthier outlook.

> *There is something about CALMING yourself and making yourself BE STILL that helps you see things in a brand-new light when you return to take up a difficult conversation where you left off.*

Psalm 46:10 says, "Be still, and know that I am God...." There is something about *calming* yourself and making yourself *be still* that helps you see things in a brand-new light when you return to take up a difficult conversation where you left off.

So whenever you're tempted to lose your peace and get into anger or strife, back off. Do whatever is needed to get your focus back to where it ought to be. Perhaps you need to read your Bible for a few minutes and allow it to produce peace in your soul. Maybe you need to find a private place so you can pray in tongues for ten minutes. Or you may be the kind of person who needs to do something physical to get rid of all that tension, such as jogging or walking.

Whatever you need to do to give yourself a few minutes of rest, do it. You'll not only feel better, but you'll be able to return to the situation at hand with renewed strength and a better perspective. By keeping yourself in check in this way, you'll protect your relationships and avoid saying harsh words in moments of weariness that you'll regret later!

SUGGESTION #2:

If you're tempted to get upset with what someone is telling you, invite a third party into the conversation so he or she can help you both hear what the other person is trying to communicate.

Sometimes when we are tempted to flare up and get into strife with someone, we are just "getting our wires crossed" and missing what that person is trying to tell us. These mishaps of misunderstanding are Satan's golden moments when he tries to wedge his way into a conversation and disrupt a relationship we cherish.

If you feel like "your feathers are getting ruffled" by something that is being said to you, it's time to use your head, tell your emotions to shut up, and invite a third party into the conversation so he or she can help you hear what is really being communicated.

I have found that the presence of an unbiased third party is often helpful. Because this person is emotionally unattached to what is happening, he or she can sometimes see the full picture more clearly than those who are in the midst of the heated discussion.

Lay down your pride and be willing to admit that you may need an objective party to help you hear more clearly.

Ephesians 4:26,27 says, "Be ye angry, and sin not: let not the sun go down upon your wrath: Neither give place to the devil." Do everything you can to stay free of anger, wrath, and strife, since these fleshly emotions give the devil free access to wage war in the situation you're facing. If bringing an unbiased person into the discussion to hear both sides helps you understand what the other person is trying to say to you, you have taken a very wise step toward disarming the devil and preventing him from doing his business!

So lay down your pride and be willing to admit that you may need an objective party to help you hear more clearly. You may be surprised to find out that you were wrong and that the other person really did have something worthy to contribute! A third person may have the very perspective you need to help you see through the muck of misunderstanding.

SUGGESTION #3:

If your conflict is with someone who is in a supervisory position over your life or work, remind yourself that you are to speak to that person with respect.

If you're tempted to get upset with your boss, pastor, or someone who holds a supervisory position over you, remind yourself that the Lord has placed him in that position. You must treat that person as someone God has placed in authority over you, even if you don't like what he is saying or doing to you at the moment. Never forget that *you* are under *him*; it isn't the other way around. If you adopt any other attitude, you'll end up being *subversive* to that God-ordained authority in your life.

You may say, "Yes, but you don't know how hard it is to work for this person!"

That may be true, but didn't you agree to submit to this situation when you took the job? If you don't like it, you may want to find another place to work or to serve. No one is making you stay where you are — *unless*, of course, the Lord has placed you there and told you it's where you're supposed to be.

"What if it's a work situation that developed after I took the job?" you may ask. Well, you can rest assured that it didn't take the Lord by surprise. Is it possible God has placed you in this position to reveal something that needs to change inside you?

> *Is it possible God has placed you in this position to reveal something that needs to change inside you?*

If the Lord has placed you there, you need to do your job with a smile on your face. Do everything in your power to go through each day with a happy heart. That may mean you have to spend more time fellowshipping with the Lord in the Word and prayer. Whatever it takes, determine that you will do it. Otherwise, you may allow your heart to become filled with scorn toward that leader and end up in rebellion against him and his orders. In that case, you would actually be rebelling against God, since He is the One who led you to take that position and work with this person in the first place!

Hebrews 13:17 says that you are to *obey* your leaders. The word "obey" is a military term that describes soldiers who know how to honor and respond to their immediate authority. It isn't the job of a soldier to correct his commanding officer. Rather, it's the soldier's responsibility to advise, help, and honor his leader by obeying his orders.

Therefore, if the person in authority over you is doing something that collides with your convictions so that you cannot follow his lead, you need to remove yourself and go somewhere else where you can work or serve with joy. Better to remove yourself from the situation than to get into strife and open a door for the devil.

Get alone with the Lord. Let the Holy Spirit speak to your heart and put the situation in right focus for you. Read and meditate on Titus 2:9: "Exhort servants to be obedient unto their own masters, and to please them well in all things; not answering again...."

Let the divine instruction in that verse sink deep in your heart. It will help you stay free from rebellion and strife when a difference of opinion arises between you and those who are in a supervisory position over you.

SUGGESTION #4:

Don't allow yourself to become a judge of another person's inward motivation.

God is the only One who sees the heart. You may think another person's actions reveal a heart that isn't right with the Lord. But you really don't know what is in that person's heart, so leave it alone. *Don't get into the judgment business.* Jesus warned us, "Judge not, that ye be

Jesus warned us, "Judge not, that ye be not judged" (Matthew 7:1). The fastest way to get a pile of judgment dumped on you is to dish it out first!

not judged" (Matthew 7:1). The fastest way to get a pile of judgment dumped on you is to dish it out first!

When you feel yourself tempted to start judging another person's inward motivations, put on the brakes and stop it as quickly as possible. Judgment results in judgment. That means you're headed in a direction that's going to bring judgment right back on your own head!

I repeat — refuse to get involved in the judgment business. Let the Lord deal with the deeper matters of someone else's heart that you can't see nor correct. Instead of getting upset with that other person, take a look in the mirror and ask yourself if you are the one who needs to change and grow up this time.

I seriously doubt that you're always right and others are always wrong. Everyone is wrong from time to time. No one is perfect in his opinion or his assessment of a situation. So it's legitimate to ask yourself: *Is a pharisaical spirit trying to operate in me — the fleshly attitude that demands to be right all the time?*

Before you start getting upset and pointing your emotional finger at others, first go take a good look at yourself. Find out if you are the one who is wrong in this particular situation.

You need some time to reassess what you're seeing, hearing, and feeling. Go to the Word of God and let its light shine into the deepest recesses of your heart so it can expose any inward wrong attitudes. Before you assume everyone else is wrong and you're right, see if you're the one who needs to change this time. It's all right to back off and let someone else be right.

So before you start getting upset and pointing your emotional finger at others, first go take a good look at yourself. Find out if *you* are the one who is wrong in this particular situation.

Suggestion #5:

Realize that your opinion is *just* your opinion.

Moral absolutes are not debatable; however, most conflicts that arise are not over moral absolutes. Most conflicts are centered around issues involving styles, choices, or mere differences of opinions.

Don't let a difference in style, choice, or opinion become bigger than it ought to be. If there are 100 people in the room, there will probably be 100 different styles, choices, or opinions about some subjects.

Stop to ask yourself, Is this really so serious? Or is this merely a difference of opinion in the minor category? Don't make a MAJOR out of a MINOR.

As long as these subjects are not important doctrinal or moral issues, don't get all bent out of shape. These are not the kinds of issues to get upset about or to fight and cause division over, so don't be guilty of "…teaching for doctrine the commandments of men" (Mark 7:7).

You have to learn to separate major issues from minor ones. Most conflicts fall within the minor category. So before your flesh becomes upset because others see things a little differently than you do, stop to ask yourself, *Is this really so serious? Or is this merely a difference of opinion in the minor category?* Don't make a *major* out of a *minor*.

<u>**SUGGESTION #6:**</u>

Learn to be flexible.

Conflicts often arise when a change occurs in one's schedule or priorities. *But change is unavoidable in life.* Every believer must develop the ability to adapt to a changing environment, for God is always telling His people, "Behold, I will do a new thing; now it shall spring forth; shall ye not know it?…" (Isaiah 43:19).

Anything that remains stagnant all the time is either dead or on the verge of dying. Tell yourself that change is not always bad. Ask the Holy Spirit to help you make the adjustments needed to "go with the flow."

Sometimes change is good for us because it forces us into a new or higher mode of thinking. We must learn to accept change as God's way of taking us to a higher level in our attitude and performance.

One thing is certain: Inflexibility leads to stress and conflict. If you are a part of an organization or a church that is experiencing growth, you'll find that it has to regularly reorganize and restructure to accommodate that growth. If you are someone who demands that everything stays the way it is right now, you'll find yourself constantly feeling upset and frustrated. It won't be too long before you are left behind in the dust.

You see, that growing organization or church will keep on growing whether you like it or not. Sadly, if you're resistant to change, the very thing you're resisting will soon outgrow you.

Of course, change just for the sake of change isn't wise because it causes instability. But change with purpose — with a justified reason that leads to a higher and better end result — will require you to do some bending and flexing in order to help bring it to pass!

Take a look at every major corporation that has touched the world, and you'll see that each one regularly updates itself so it can remain viable in today's market. Any corporation that refuses to do this will be overtaken by its competitors and will lose the edge it once held.

For instance, I remember back when the electric typewriter first came on the scene. It was a marvel of technology to the world's typing population. Then computers were introduced to the general public. That really made waves in the business world!

To adapt to the new computer technology, people had to learn how to let go of the past to embrace the present. Imagine what the world would be like today if the business community had refused to leave their electric typewriters behind! For the world to be interconnected as it is today, it was essential for people to embrace a *change*.

If you can't handle the changes that go along with growth, it would be better for you to go join another organization or church that is satisfied with the status quo. Maybe it just isn't in your heart to be a leader. You'd rather stick with the old ways of doing things.

But if you choose to move forward and take a proactive approach to life, you must ask the Holy Spirit to help you make the adjustments needed to "go with the flow." You also must believe that God is truly able to direct those who are in authority over you.

If the situation you're in has revealed inflexibility in your character, it's already been a good experience for you. It has shown you where you need to develop and mature so you can achieve what God has called you to do.

If the situation you're in has revealed inflexibility in your character, it's already been a good experience for you. It has shown you where you need to develop and mature so you can achieve what God has called you to do. Rather than feeling threatened, you can choose to see that He is working to change you. If you take this approach — if you choose to look for and find the hand of God in the situation — it will remove any threat you may feel.

Suggestion #7:

Give others the benefit of the doubt.

People often act in a way that is misperceived by others. Maybe they don't realize how their actions are being perceived and therefore project attitudes or actions that are contrary to what they actually intend.

Have you ever been misunderstood? Has anyone ever called your motives into question? Did it shock you to hear what others misperceived about you, especially when you knew your intentions were right?

This happens to everyone from time to time. Just as you want others to believe the best about you, it's important for you to reverse that grace and believe the best about others. Jesus gave us this principle in Luke 6:31 when He said, "...As ye would that men should do to you, do ye also to them likewise."

So when an offense occurs, assume that the person didn't intend to be offensive. Give the same grace to others that you want others to extend to you. Give them the benefit of a doubt. Mercy is never wrong.

> *Give the same grace to others that you want others to extend to you. Give them the benefit of a doubt. Mercy is never wrong.*

SUGGESTION #8:

Be forgiving when others act ugly.

When someone rubs you the wrong way and you're tempted to get offended or upset because of that person's flaws, remember how often God has had patience with your *own* flaws and faults.

Before you become too condemning, put the situation in the right perspective. Ask yourself, *Have I ever acted ugly or spoken an unkind word?* Chances are that you've done the very same thing to others that this person you're upset with has done to you!

Speak to your emotions when you're tempted to get offended or to get into strife. Remind yourself to accept others just as Jesus Christ has freely and graciously accepted you.

Romans 15:7 says, "Wherefore receive ye one another, as Christ also received us to the glory of God." How did Jesus receive you and me? Did He require perfection of us first, or did He take us just as we were at the time we came to Him? Praise God, He took us just as we were, with all our attitude problems, defects, inconsistencies, and blemishes!

Since you've been saved, have you ever done anything to disappoint the Lord? Have you ever allowed yourself to act in a manner that was unbecoming for a Christian? Have you ever entertained ugly thoughts or accusations about someone else?

Yes, of course you have. Yet Jesus has never cast you away or become so disgusted that He's disowned you.

According to Romans 15:7, we are to receive each other just as Christ has received us. That means we need to do a lot of forgiving and overlooking in life!

I strongly advise you to quit focusing on the faults and flaws of others, and start concentrating on how to be more forgiving and merciful. If you give mercy, you'll receive a harvest of mercy in your own life.

Take the route of mercy, and you'll never be sorry. Believe it or not, there are times when you're supposed to shut your eyes to what you saw that other person do and just let it go!

If you give mercy, you'll receive a harvest of mercy in your own life.

If you'll take this approach to life, you'll have a lot less emotional disappointments and problems with your nerves. Just give people the same forgiveness and mercy you want others to extend to you.

SUGGESTION #9:

Ask yourself: *Would I want someone else to respond to me in the same way I am responding right now?*

When my flesh wants to rant and rave about an injustice it thinks has been done to it, I am tempted to be very bold and aggressive with my offenders. This is usually the time when unkind words are spoken or extreme statements are made that get all blown out of proportion.

When I am tempted to get upset, I ask myself, *If this situation were turned around and someone was upset with ME, would I want that person to react to me in this attitude?* Of course, the answer is *no*!

> *Ask yourself, Do my attitudes and actions reflect the esteem and honor I would like to receive from others if the situation was reversed and I was the recipient of a deserved rebuke?*

In Philippians 2:3, Paul tells us, "Let nothing be done through strife or vainglory; but in lowliness of mind let each esteem other better than themselves." When dealing with another person, always go the route of preferring and esteeming that person better than yourself. As you do, you'll rarely speak an unkind word or allow your flesh to rant and rave.

Ask yourself, *Do my attitudes and actions reflect the esteem and honor I would like to receive from others if the situation was reversed and I was the recipient of a deserved rebuke?*

SUGGESTION #10:

What would Jesus do in this situation? What instruction has the Holy Spirit given you?

Jesus went to the Cross and died for those who hung Him! He could have called 12 legions of angels to come to His defense; instead, "…he threatened not; but committed himself to him that judgeth righteously" (1 Peter 2:23).

Is it possible that you need to keep your mouth shut and follow in the steps of Jesus this time (*see* 1 Peter 2:21)?

Most often it is better to go the way of the Cross and allow God to be your Defender. Of course, you must deal with problems when they arise, especially if they are of a severe nature. But never forget that God is a God of justice. Let Him be the Defender of your dreams and ideas.

> *Never forget that God is a God of justice. Let Him be the Defender of your dreams and ideas.*

The Holy Spirit may show you other ways to shut the door to resentment, offense, bitterness, and strife. If you will listen to Him, He will show you how to circumvent the attacks the enemy tries to wage in your soul against your family, friends, and fellow workers.

If you refuse to listen to the Holy Spirit, you can expect grudges, resentments, hostilities, animosities, and anger to begin building up inside you with every unresolved conflict and added offense. In the end, your bitter, angry attitudes will separate you from the people you normally get along with and dearly love.

When Satan's "hook" is firmly set, those lies and wrong emotions will become a stronghold in your life. You'll begin to rationalize and find logical justifications for holding on to those killer attitudes — even though you know they are wrong.

Don't let Satan sink his hook in you through offense! Follow in the footsteps of Jesus, and go the way of the Cross. It may seem painfully difficult at the moment, but I guarantee you that it isn't as painful as a heart full of bitterness, resentment, and strife!

So What Are You Going To Do?

No matter what hurt or offense you've experienced in the past, your refusal to forgive the other person isn't worth the pain or bondage that unforgiveness will produce in your life. After all, why should you add pain and distress to your life by holding on to bitterness? Why let the memory of a wound or of a suffered loss stalk and torment your mind and emotions any longer?

You can singlehandedly hinder or even forfeit the future blessings God has ordained for you if you persist in holding fast to bitterness and pain.

God wants to give you bright hope for a new future (Jeremiah 29:11). However, you can singlehandedly hinder or even forfeit the future blessings God has ordained for you if you persist in holding fast to bitterness and pain. Someone may have wronged you in the past, or you may be in the middle of a painful situation right now. But you don't have to let *anyone's* actions against you pollute your present attitude or prevent God's good plan for your future. How you choose to respond to offense today will determine what direction your life will take in the days to come.

No harbored offense is worth sabotaging your future. The devil is counting on you to walk after the flesh rather than after the Spirit so he can derail your destiny. But he can't thwart what God has for you without your permission and participation.

Offense is nothing more than a trap — a trap you can avoid as long as you refuse to hold on to it. So when offense is hurled at you, *let it go*. When you do, you'll walk away *free* — free to be all God intended for you to be as you pursue the destiny God ordained exclusively for your life.

Once you've made the choice to grab hold of God's grace and let Him take you over those emotional hurdles, don't ever let the devil drag you back into the bondage of bitterness and offense again. Stay free!

Once you've made the choice to grab hold of God's grace and let Him take you over those emotional hurdles, don't ever let the devil drag you back into the bondage of bitterness and offense again. *Stay free!* It's time to rise up and take charge of the situation in your soul.

Remember, it's *your* soul, and you are responsible for what happens there.

The Holy Spirit is present right now to help you make the choice to forgive and forget. You can permanently walk free of what others have done to you — or what you *think* they did to you.

It doesn't matter who was right or wrong in the situation. What matters is that you uproot the tree of bitterness before it begins producing deadly fruit in your life. If other believers really did commit an offense against you, God will deal with them. After all, they are His children too.

So ask the Holy Spirit today to come alongside you and help you turn from those feelings of bitterness and unforgiveness. Then expect Him to empower you so you can speak with authority to the bitterness that has kept you bound for too long. Tell that bitterness to go in Jesus' name — and then begin to walk free from offense once and for all!

Think About It

God wants your heart free from both the burden and the pain of offense. What has He spoken to your heart as you read this book? Which of the ten suggestions in this chapter addressed the specific actions you know you need to take right now to step into freedom?

When you look to Jesus with a confident expectation of His help, He will strengthen you with His grace, and His power will undergird you wherever you are weak.

Hebrews 12:1,2 (*NLT*) sets your focus squarely where it must remain as you embark on your own personal path toward a lifetime of freedom from offense: "...Let us strip off every weight that slows us down, especially the sin that so easily trips us up. And let us run with endurance the race God has set before us. We do this by *keeping our eyes on Jesus*, the champion who initiates and perfects our faith." *Think about it.*

Prayer of Forgiveness

No one is spared opportunities for offense in this life. Not one person escapes times of dealing with disappointments or hurt as the result of other people's words or actions. But as you've read the pages of this book, you've seen that it's *how you respond* to hurt, betrayal, or offense that makes all the difference in the outcome — both in your life and the life of your offender.

Please take the time to pray this prayer from your heart:

Dear Heavenly Father,

I thank You for the great love You expressed when You sent Jesus to be my Savior, my Substitute, and my Example. As I look at Jesus' life and His responses to all that He experienced, I see Your heart and mind revealed. Thank You, Father, for loving me so completely and for forgiving me so fully.

Right now, Father, I come before You as humbly and as sincerely as I know how to honor You for the great sacrifice of Your Son. I honor You by acknowledging and receiving the power of the blood that Jesus so willingly shed for the forgiveness and removal of my sins. And just as I require and receive the power of that precious blood in my life, I release its cleansing power through forgiveness toward those who have hurt or wronged me in the past.

Father, as an act of my will, I choose to believe and act upon Your Word that tells me to forgive. I know that You said great peace belongs to those who love Your law and that nothing shall offend them (Psalm 119:165). I feel the sting of betrayal, but I'm not ignorant of the enemy's devices. The purpose of betrayal is to produce a root of bitterness in me, and I refuse to yield to that sin. Father, I forgive — and I also ask You to forgive those who have hurt me, for they don't know what they're doing. They don't realize that what has been said and done against me has been said and done against You. Forgive them, Father.

Holy Spirit, I ask You to help me yield to the love of God that has already been shed abroad in my heart by Your presence within me. As You strengthened Jesus, please strengthen me. Help me walk in the love, the Word, and the will of God toward those who have wronged me. Help me respond just as Jesus responded when He was spitefully treated and wrongfully accused. I take comfort and find strength in Jesus' example before me and in Your mighty presence within me, Holy Spirit. Help me lean upon You without reservation and to respond to You without hesitation. And help those I have forgiven to turn their hearts toward You. May we both embrace Your wisdom and Your ways so that Your purpose may be fulfilled in each of our lives.

Thank You, Father, for the blood of Jesus that has the power to cleanse sin and to remove barriers. I ask that You intervene in our hearts and in this situation to turn all that the enemy meant for evil toward our good and Your glory. I receive this as done in Jesus' name. Amen.

REFERENCE BOOK LIST

1. *How To Use New Testament Greek Study Aids* by Walter Jerry Clark (Loizeaux Brothers).

2. *Strong's Exhaustive Concordance of the Bible* by James H. Strong.

3. *The Interlinear Greek-English New Testament* by George Ricker Berry (Baker Book House).

4. *The Englishman's Greek Concordance of the New Testament* by George Wigram (Hendrickson).

5. *New Thayer's Greek-English Lexicon of the New Testament* by Joseph Thayer (Hendrickson).

6. *The Expanded Vine's Expository Dictionary of New Testament Words* by W. E. Vine (Bethany).

7. *Theological Dictionary of the New Testament* by Geoffrey Bromiley; Gephard Kittle, ed. (Eerdmans).

8. *The New Analytical Greek Lexicon*; Wesley Perschbacher, ed. (Hendrickson).

9. *The New Linguistic and Exegetical Key to the Greek New Testament* by Cleon Rogers Jr. (Zondervan).

10. *Word Studies in the Greek New Testament* by Kenneth Wuest, 4 Volumes (Eerdmans).

11. *New Testament Words* by William Barclay (Westminster Press).

12. *Word Meanings* by Ralph Earle (Hendrickson).

13. *International Critical Commentary Series*; J. A. Emerton, C. E. B. Cranfield, and G. N. Stanton, eds. (T. & T. Clark International).

14. *Vincent's Word Studies of the New Testament* by Marvin R. Vincent, 4 Volumes (Hendrickson).

15. *New International Dictionary of New Testament Theology*; Verlyn D. Verbrugge, ed. (Zondervan).

ABOUT THE AUTHOR

Rick Renner is a prolific author and a highly respected Bible teacher and leader in the international Christian community. Rick is the author of more than 30 books, including the bestsellers *Dressed To Kill* and *Sparkling Gems From the Greek*, all of which have sold more than 3 million copies combined. In 1991, Rick and his family moved to what is now the former Soviet Union. Today he is the senior pastor of the *Moscow Good News Church*; the founder and director of the *Good News Association of Pastors and Churches*, with a membership of several hundred churches; and the founder of *Media Mir*, the first Christian television network in the former USSR that today broadcasts the Gospel to a potential audience of 100 million people and to countless Russian-speaking viewers around the world via multiple satellites. Rick's wife and lifelong ministry partner, Denise, and their three sons — Paul, Philip, and Joel — lead this amazing work with the help of their committed leadership team. Rick and Denise, along with their sons and families, all reside in Moscow.

A WORD ABOUT OUR WORK

From inception to its current role in the Body of Christ, *RENNER Ministries'* purpose and vision has been to teach, strengthen, and rescue people for the Kingdom of God. Although the Renners' ministry began much earlier, in 1991 God called Rick and Denise Renner and their family to what is now the former Soviet Union. Since that time, millions of lives have been touched by the various outreaches of *RENNER Ministries*. Nevertheless, the Renners' ever-increasing vision for this region of the world continues to expand across 9 time zones to reach 300 million precious souls for God's Kingdom.

The *Moscow Good News Church* was begun in September 2000 in the very heart of Moscow, right next to Red Square. Since that time, the church has grown to become one of the largest Protestant churches in Moscow and a strategic model for pastors throughout this region of the world to learn from and emulate. Today outreaches include ministry to families, senior citizens, children, youth, international church members, specialized ministry to businesspeople, and an outreach to the poor and needy. Rick and Denise also founded churches in Riga, Latvia, and in Kiev, Ukraine, both of which continue to thrive.

Part of the mission of *RENNER Ministries* is to come alongside pastors and ministers and take them to a higher level of excellence and professionalism in the ministry. Therefore, since 1991 when the walls of Communism first collapsed, this ministry has been working in the former USSR to train and equip pastors, church leaders, and ministers, helping them attain the necessary skills and knowledge to fulfill the ministries that the Lord has given them.

To this end, Rick Renner founded both a ministry training center and a ministerial association. The *Good News Training Center* operates as a part of the *Moscow Good News Church*. It specializes in training leaders to start new churches all over the former Soviet Union. The *Good News Association of Pastors and Churches* is a church-planting and church-supporting organization with a membership of pastors and churches that numbers in the hundreds.

Rick and Denise Renner also oversee *Media Mir*, the first and one of the largest TV outreaches within the territory of the former USSR. Since its inception in 1992, this television network has become one of the strongest instruments available today for declaring the Word of God to the 15 nations of the former Soviet Union, reaching 100 million potential viewers every day with the Gospel of Jesus Christ. The network also reaches an untold number of Russian speakers on almost every continent of the world via satellite.

The Renners also founded the *"It's Possible"* humanitarian foundation, which is involved in various outreaches in the city of Moscow. The *"It's Possible"* foundation uses innovative methods to help different age groups of people who are in great need.

In addition to conducting their work in the former Soviet Union, Rick and Denise Renner continue to expand their outreach throughout the world. They are teaching God's Word to people in the United States through a variety of means: producing books and audio resources; conducting meetings in churches, seminars, and conferences throughout the country; and appearing frequently on nationwide TV programs, such as *Believer's Voice of Victory* with Kenneth Copeland, *Enjoying Everyday Life* with Joyce Meyer, *700 Club* with Pat Robertson, and *Life Today* with James Robison. The Renners also reach out to English-speaking people around the globe through their eBooks and MP3 audio teachings; their online IMPART network, designed to help ministers; their various Internet video programs; and the meetings they conduct in other nations around the world.

If you would like to learn more about the many aspects and outreaches of *RENNER Ministries*, please visit our website at www.renner.org, or call 918-496-3213.

A NOTE TO BOOKSELLERS

For all wholesale book orders,
please contact:

A book company anointed to take God's Word
to you and to the nations of the world.

A Division of
Rick Renner Ministries
P. O. Box 702040
Tulsa, OK 74170-2040
Phone: 877-281-8644
Fax: 918-496-3278
Email: tan@renner.org
Website: www.tanpublish.com

FOR FURTHER INFORMATION

For additional copies of this book
or for further information
about this ministry and other Renner products,
please contact the RENNER Ministries office nearest you,
or visit the ministry website at **www.renner.org**.
(**Note:** For online orders, digital downloads are available.
All physical product orders are available only in the U.S.
If outside the U.S., please contact
a RENNER Ministries office near you.)

ALL USA CORRESPONDENCE:
RENNER Ministries
P. O. Box 702040
Tulsa, OK 74170-2040
(918) 496-3213
Or 1-800-RICK-593
Email: renner@renner.org
Website: www.renner.org

MOSCOW OFFICE:
RENNER Ministries
P. O. Box 53
Moscow 109316, Russia
7 (495) 727-1470
Email: mirpress@umail.ru
Website: www.mgnc.org

Riga Office:
RENNER Ministries
Unijas 99
Riga LV-1084, Latvia
(371) 780-2150
Email: info@goodnews.lv

Kiev Office:
RENNER Ministries
P. O. Box 146
Kiev 01025, Ukraine
380 (44) 246-6552
Email: mirpress@rrm.kiev.ua

Oxford Office:
RENNER Ministries
Box 7, 266 Banbury Road
Oxford OX2 7DL, England
44 (1865) 355509
Email: europe@renner.org

A LIGHT IN DARKNESS
VOLUME ONE

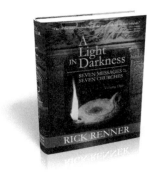

Step into the world of the First Century Church as Rick Renner creates a panoramic experience of unsurpassed detail to transport you into the ancient lands of the seven churches of Asia Minor. Within the context of this fascinating — and, at times, shocking — historical backdrop, Rick outlines challenges early believers faced in taking the Gospel to a pagan world. After presenting a riveting account of the apostle John's vision of the exalted Christ, Rick leads you through an in-depth study of Jesus' messages to the churches of Ephesus and Smyrna — profoundly relevant messages that still resonate for His Church today.

$79.95 (Hardback)
ISBN 978-0-9779459-8-6

Rick's richly detailed historical narrative, enhanced by classic artwork and superb photographs shot on location at archeological sites, will make the lands and the message of the Bible come alive to you as never before. Parallels between Roman society of the First Century and the modern world prove the current relevance of Christ's warnings and instructions.

A Light in Darkness is an extraordinary book series that will endure and speak to generations to come. This authoritative first volume is a virtual encyclopedia of knowledge — a definitive *go-to* resource for any student of the Bible and a classic *must-have* for Christian families everywhere.

Faced with daunting challenges, the modern Church *must* give urgent heed to what the Holy Spirit is saying in order to be equipped for the end of this age.

For more information, visit us online at: **www.renner.org**
Book Resellers: Contact Teach All Nations at 877-281-8644,
or email **tan@renner.org** for quantity discounts.

MINING THE TREASURES
OF GOD'S WORD

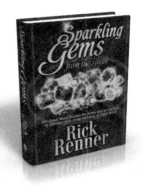

Author Rick Renner unearths a rich treasure trove of truths in his remarkable devotional, ***Sparkling Gems From the Greek***. Drawing from an extensive study of both the Bible and New Testament Greek, Rick illuminates 365 passages with more than 1,285 in-depth Greek word studies. Far from intellectualizing, he blends his solid instruction with practical applications and refreshing insights. Find challenge, reassurance, comfort, and reminders of God's abiding love and healing every day of the year.

$34.95 (Hardback)
ISBN: 978-0-9725454-2-6

Sparkling Gems From the Greek
Electronic Reference Edition

Now you are only a few short clicks away from discovering the untold riches of God's Word! Offering embedded links to three exhaustive indices for ultimate ease in cross-referencing scriptures and Greek word studies, this unique computer study tool gives you both convenience and portability as you read and explore Rick Renner's one-of-a-kind daily devotional!

$29.95 (CD-ROM)
ISBN: 978-0-9725454-7-1

For more information, visit us online at: **www.renner.org**
Book Resellers: Contact Teach All Nations at 877-281-8644,
or email **tan@renner.org** for quantity discounts.

A BIBLICAL APPROACH TO SPIRITUAL WARFARE

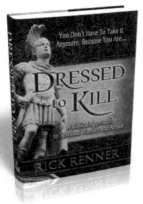

Rick Renner's book *Dressed To Kill* is considered by many to be a true classic on the subject of spiritual warfare. The original version, which sold more than 400,000 copies, is a curriculum staple in Bible schools worldwide. In this beautifully bound hardback volume, you will find:

- 512 pages of reedited text

- 16 pages of full-color illustrations

- Questions at the end of each chapter to guide you into deeper study

$24.95 (Hardback)
ISBN: 978-0-9779459-0-0

In *Dressed To Kill*, Rick explains with exacting detail the purpose and function of each piece of Roman armor. In the process, he describes the significance of our *spiritual* armor not only to withstand the onslaughts of the enemy, but also to overturn the tendencies of the carnal mind. Furthermore, Rick delivers a clear, scriptural presentation on the biblical definition of spiritual warfare — what it is and what it is not.

When you walk with God in deliberate, continual fellowship, He will enrobe you with Himself. Armed with the knowledge of who you are in Him, you will be dressed and dangerous to the works of darkness, unflinching in the face of conflict, and fully equipped to take the offensive and gain mastery over any opposition from your spiritual foe. You don't have to accept defeat anymore once you are *dressed to kill!*

For more information, visit us online at: **www.renner.org**
Book Resellers: Contact Teach All Nations at 877-281-8644,
or email **tan@renner.org** for quantity discounts.

BOOKS BY RICK RENNER

*Digital version available for Kindle, Nook, iBook, and other eBook formats.

Note: For audio and video teaching materials by Rick Renner, please visit **www.renner.org**.

Books in Russian

Dream Thieves

Dressed To Kill

The Dynamic Duo

Good News About Your New Life

If You Were God, Would You Choose You?

Insights to Successful Leadership

You Can Get Over It

Hell Is a Real Place

How To Test Spiritual Manifestations

A Light in Darkness, Volume One

Living in the Combat Zone

Merchandising the Anointing

Paid in Full

The Point of No Return

Seducing Spirits and Doctrines of Demons

Sparkling Gems From the Greek Daily Devotional

Spiritual Weapons To Defeat the Enemy

Ten Guidelines To Help You Achieve
  Your Long-Awaited Promotion!

365 Days of Power

What the Bible Says About Healing

What the Bible Says About Tithes and Offerings

What the Bible Says About Water Baptism

What To Do if You've Had a Failure

Study Notes

Study Notes

Study Notes

Study Notes

Study Notes